VISUAL DELIGHTS

VISUAL DELIGHTS

Nathalie Hambro

with photographs by Christine Hanscomb

Little, Brown and Company

BOSTON TORONTO

To my husband, *in toto*

First published in 1985 in Great Britain by Conran Octopus Limited.

Conceived, designed and produced by
Conran Octopus Limited
28-32 Shelton Street
London WC2 9PH

Library of Congress Catalog Card No. 85-82202
First U.S. Edition

Printed in Italy

FOREWORD

When I left Paris some fourteen years ago, good eating was a part of my life that I took for granted. The London shops then were quite a come-down compared with the *marché du quartier* with its bounty of fresh-looking and delicious wares. Being newly married, it seemed important to me that our relationship should be sustained with something more wholesome than 'fast' food. Good food became an obsession which had to be dealt with and delicious meals were the focal point of family and friendly gatherings.

While I was having a little revolution in my own kitchen, discovering English and ethnic cooking, France was being hit by Nouvelle Cuisine. Such was the rage that it was inescapable.

During that period the most worthwhile cookery advance was the emphasis given to first-rate ingredients simply presented without the usual disguise of over-elaborate sauces. In other words, the creation of simple recipes with quite sophisticated or unusual combinations of ingredients. By trial and error I probably went too far from time to time, but that was all part of the experimentation a self-taught cook so enjoys.

English kitchen gardens were a new discovery for me, giving me the opportunity to try unusual herbs which were common in Elizabethan times, for example, and root vegetables which are sadly so underrated in France. The fishmonger, too, had arrays of fish little known in France. By combining the French and English attitudes towards food, and taking in Indian and Asian cuisine, I developed some intriguing ideas in which presentation played a large part. For me, the art of eating extends far beyond the mere techniques of cookery. The appearance of the food is crucially important since it triggers off the imagination and heightens the anticipation of the pleasure of eating. Hunting through antique and junk shops for interesting pieces of china, cutlery, utensils and fabrics for the table was a related and enjoyable exercise since the table setting and the surroundings – including flowers, pictures, ornaments and music – play an important role in creating a pleasant environment.

If you have only a little time in which to organize and prepare a dinner party do not be over ambitious; you will be too harassed to enjoy the company of your guests. Much of the success of a meal is dependent upon the hostess being relaxed and by calmly offering your guests simple but beautifully presented food in pleasant surroundings, the meal can only be a success.

Spontaneity is my rule for planning meals – deciding what looks the most interesting and inspiring in the market and the shops, always buying what is in season. Reading old cookery books helped me become more original and flexible in my cooking. Also, doing all the work in the kitchen myself, informality is the order of the day – so no set menus with a starter and main course, but a combination of both using a balance of textures, colours and, of course, flavours. I like the Chinese idea of clusters of food rather than courses, serving many dishes that can be sampled in varying proportions. Approximate servings are given at the end of each recipe, and, with the exception of 'individual' portions, there is usually as much flexibility in that number as there is in the combination of dishes being served. For example, a meal of six dishes will serve more guests than one of four dishes. Therefore, if one dish specifies six servings and another specifies four, this is not objectively wrong but merely a question of portion sizes. An experienced cook/hostess can sense if the chosen combination of dishes will be generous enough.

In this book the recipes are firstly organized according to season because the quality of the raw ingredients is of prime importance and the seasons dictate the choice of the freshest and most delicious ingredients available. Each season is then subdivided into the following sections: Eggs, Cheeses and Grains; Fish and Shellfish; Meat, Poultry and Game; Vegetables and Salads; Sauces; Desserts and Cakes; and Drinks. Feel free to cross seasons as there is no really hard and fast line restricting availability exactly to a particular season, though certain ingredients are highly seasonal. But here is a challenge for the adventurous cook to substitute ingredients, spices or herbs which are more easily available, or which take her fancy. Cooking should be creative and sometimes restricted access to ingredients leads to original and imaginative results. Most of the recipes in this book need not be followed literally, thereby allowing a certain amount of flexibility.

Some artistic licence was taken when we prepared the food for the photographic sessions. Most shots were taken of finished dishes but some were of the ingredients, others were only partially prepared, and in a few the final quantities were slightly altered in sympathy with the culinary image.

In each photograph we tried to create a different mood, reflecting the appropriate season, and combining complementary flavours, textures and images.

I hope that in producing this book I have achieved a visual awareness that goes beyond the usual bounds of cookery.

NATHALIE HAMBRO

CONTENTS

SPRING

SUMMER

CONTENTS

AUTUMN

WINTER

SPRING

Spring means the gradual re-emergence of green after a cold grey winter. Fresh, leafy growth fills the garden and young, tender vegetables become, as the season progresses, the most valuable raw material in the kitchen. Treatment of vegetables changes, from the slow, lengthy cooking and puréeing of stored winter root vegetables, towards the simplest and most direct presentation of the freshest possible produce. Spring vegetables are tender enough to be served raw, small enough to be served whole, while lightly steamed they offer additional possibilities. With vegetables come the sauces of spring, the rich, creamy mayonnaises and yoghurt dressings that introduce pastel tones and serve as a soft, smooth complement to salads, and their sweet counterparts that enliven desserts and puddings.

The anticipation of the heat of summer, and the reality of the hot, sunny days of late spring, place frozen desserts firmly on the menu. Frozen creams, ices, sorbets and ice creams continue the theme of pastel colours, subtle flavours. And because most can be made well in advance, they demand little attention when they are really needed – when an afternoon turns unexpectedly hot and sunny; when friends stop by for a meal . . .

As spring progresses and, hopefully, weather improves, the location and patterns of dining respond. The transitional environments of conservatories, sun rooms, sheltered courtyards and patios, replace the inward-looking, totally enclosed dining room and kitchen. These spring venues provide the best of both worlds – exposure to the visual delights of the garden in spring and protection from the unpredictable and often fickle spring weather. Masses of cut flowers or even potted plants, bridge the gap between indoors and out, whether your garden is as lush as the one illustrated or virtually nonexistent.

Eggs, Cheeses and Grains

SCRAMBLED EGGS AUX DEUX VERDURES

What is intriguing about this recipe is that the same
vegetable – spinach in this instance – is used in two
different forms: cooked and raw. The cooked spinach
could be replaced with steamed beetroot leaves. For a
richer, heavier texture, add a tablespoon of cream to the
scrambled eggs towards the end of cooking. Serve with
Palia e Fieno Salad, p26.

olive oil
2 oz (60 g) butter
8 eggs
freshly grated nutmeg
salt and white pepper
a few chives, finely chopped
1½ lb (675 g) young spinach

Scrupulously clean the spinach, removing the stalks. Heat the olive oil in a
large, enamelled pan and add two-thirds of the spinach (reserving the younger
ones), with water still clinging to the leaves. Cover and steam-fry for 4 to 5
minutes, giving one stir with a wooden spoon. Season with nutmeg, salt and
pepper. Reserve.

Thoroughly dry the remaining spinach leaves and chop them roughly.
Sprinkle with salt and pepper. Reserve.

In a heavy saucepan, melt the butter until it reaches the 'noisette' stage,
which means when a nutty aroma escapes from the pan. Reduce the heat and
immediately pour in the lightly beaten eggs (scrambled eggs shouldn't have
the whites and yolks totally mixed) seasoned with nutmeg, salt and pepper.
Stir constantly with a wooden spoon, until the eggs are evenly set, but not firm.
Add some of the finely chopped chives and transfer immediately to a dish to
stop the cooking process, which would continue in the hot saucepan.

To assemble: using a flat round dish, put the scrambled eggs, in a mound,
in the centre. Then place the cooked spinach around the mound in a crown-like
fashion. Surround with raw spinach and sprinkle with the remaining chopped
chives. Serve hot or at room temperature.

Serves 4

*Scrambled Eggs aux Deux Verdures, Palia
e Fieno Salad*

Egg and Sorrel Cup, Arab Bread Rolls,
Poussins with Kumquats

EGG AND SORREL CUP

Watercress or spinach could be substituted for the sorrel.
Serve with Arab Bread Rolls and Poussins with
Kumquats, p22.

Per person
1 soft-boiled egg
4-6 sorrel leaves
4 fl oz (120 ml) yoghurt
mace
salt and freshly ground pepper

Remove most of the stalks from the sorrel leaves and shred in long ribbons.
Season the yoghurt with mace, salt and pepper, and beat it until smooth. Add
the sorrel. Place the egg carefully at the bottom of a cup, soup bowl or ramekin,
and cover with the sauce. Serve at room temperature.

ARAB BREAD ROLLS

Arab bread is similar to Greek Pitta bread. Here it is filled
with a thin herb omelette and a slice of tongue.

3 Arab breads
5 eggs
1 tablespoon milk
1 handful fresh coriander or parsley, chopped
1 tablespoon butter
6 tongue slices
salt and freshly ground pepper
6-8 sprigs of fresh coriander or parsley

Heat the breads in a warm oven for 2 minutes and then slit open the breads into
halves. Reserve. In a bowl, beat the eggs, milk and parsley or coriander, and
season. In a small omelette pan, melt a little butter and add some of the egg
mixture. Make a thin omelette cooked on one side only. When cooked, place it
on the cut side of a bread half. Make 5 more omelettes, greasing the pan each
time, and placing each omelette on a bread half. Put a tongue slice on each and
roll up, securing it with a 'saté' or cocktail stick. Grill for 1 minute, tuck in
coriander or parsley for garnish and serve.

Serves 6

Eggs, Cheeses and Grains

GREEN PANCAKES WITH RICOTTA

These pancakes are equally good eaten cold; they go well
with the Jambon Persillade, p21.

3 red chicory (radicchio)

Batter	**Filling**
4 oz (120 g) finely chopped frozen spinach	*12 oz (340 g) ricotta cheese*
4 oz (120 g) plain white flour	*1 egg white*
1 large egg	*a pinch bicarbonate of soda*
10 fl oz (280 ml) milk	*1 teaspoon fresh tarragon*
mace	*or ½ teaspoon dried tarragon*
salt and freshly ground pepper	*salt and freshly ground pepper*
oil or butter	

Preheat the oven 350°F/180°C/Gas 4

Cook the spinach until most of the moisture has evaporated. Reserve.

In a large bowl, make the batter in the usual way; beat the flour, egg, milk
and seasoning, then add the spinach and ensure that no lumps remain. Leave
for about an hour to allow the flour to swell. I normally use two 8 in (20 cm)
frying pans to make the pancakes. Brush the pans with a little oil or butter
every other pancake, working simultaneously with the two pans. Stack the
green pancakes on a flat plate, placing between each one a square of greaseproof
paper or foil. Cover the top pancake with a piece of foil to keep them moist.

In a bowl, lightly beat the ricotta, using a fork. In another bowl, firmly beat
the egg white with a pinch each of bicarbonate of soda and salt. With a spatula
fold the beaten egg white into the ricotta mixture, adding the tarragon, salt and
freshly ground pepper.

Brush an ovenproof dish with butter. Place a little of the filling over one
quarter of a pancake and fold in four. Place on the dish. Repeat the operation
with the other pancakes, dot the dish with butter and cover tightly with foil.
(Up to this stage the recipe may be prepared ahead of time.) Heat the spinach
pancakes for 20-30 minutes.

Serve on a flat serving dish lined with shredded red chicory or shredded
lettuce, or a white napkin.

Makes 12 pancakes

ELDERFLOWER BREAD

This light wholesome bread is delicately flavoured with
elderflowers and lemon. I use it to make thin toast which I
serve with soup or to make cream-cheese sandwiches with
one or two dried figs pressed in. It makes a nice
accompaniment to salads of any sort. The fresh
elderflowers may be replaced here with 1 heaped
tablespoon dried ones, available from herbalists.

1 teaspoon dried yeast
1 teaspoon coarse sea salt
10 fl oz (280 ml) buttermilk or milk, warmed
about 1¾ lb (550 g) strong white flour
3-4 fresh elderflower heads or 1 heaped tablespoon of dried
flowers
grated rind of 1 lemon
oil for greasing

Stir the yeast in 2 tablespoons warm water and leave for 10 minutes or until
frothy. Add the salt to the buttermilk or milk, and stir until dissolved. Strip the
elderflowers from their stalks. In a large bowl, put the flour, elderflowers, and
lemon rind, then add the yeast mixture and buttermilk or milk. Stir to blend,
then knead for a minute or two. Leave the dough covered with a polythene bag,
to rise, in a warm place, until doubled in bulk. This should take about 1 hour.

With your fist, punch down the dough to release the air and reduce it to its
initial volume. Knead for 7-10 minutes. Grease 2 small bread tins. Divide the
dough in two and put it in the tins. Invert and replace the dough, upside-down
in the tins, so that the greased bottoms are on top. Cover with the polythene
bag and leave to rise for a second time for 2-3 hours.

Preheat the oven to 400°F/200°C/Gas 6. Place a metal tray filled with water,
on the bottom shelf; the steam will give the bread a crispy crust. Bake for 45
minutes. Remove the loaves from the tins and leave them to cool, upside-
down, on a rack.

Makes 2 small loaves

STEAMED SEA BREAM

Here the fish is steamed in a Chinese bamboo steamer into which a heatproof glass pie dish has been fitted. Choose the freshest fish possible, with bright red gills. The fish should be cleaned and scaled, and the fin removed, but with the head and tail intact.

about 1¹/₂ lb (675 g) sea bream or bass
1 teaspoon sesame oil
¹/₂ teaspoon coarse sea salt
2 teaspoons soya sauce
2 in (5 cm) fresh ginger root
6 spring onions

The pie dish should be about 1 in (2.5 cm) smaller than the steamer, to allow the steam to reach the fish. Grease it lightly with some of the sesame oil and place it in the steamer.

Clean and pat dry the fish. Holding it tightly with a cloth, score with 3 crosswise diagonal slices on each side. Use a sharp knife, and cut nearly to the bone. Sprinkle with sea salt and rub it into the score marks.

Peel and cut 2.5 cm (1 in) of ginger root into thin slices, then in long strands. Peel and slice the remaining ginger into thin oval slices. Cut 5 spring onions in half, lengthways, and cut the remaining spring onions into julienne strips in a greased pie dish, arrange the spring onion halves and ginger slices in a fan-like pattern, then place the bream on top. Mix the soya sauce and the remaining sesame oil and spoon over the bream, then scatter over the ginger strands and julienne strips of spring onion. Tightly fit the steamer over a pan or wok filled with boiling water and steam the fish for 10-12 minutes, depending on its thickness. Do not overcook.

With heatproof gloves on, remove the steamer from the heat, and transfer the fish to a serving dish. Divide into helpings, following the score marks, and spoon over a little of the liquor.

Serves 4

Partially prepared Steamed Sea Bream

Fish

RAINBOW TROUT SALAD

Cucumber, p27, and Spinach and Chicken Salad
Chinese Style, p23. It is important to get very fresh trout
as they are 'cooked' only by the marinade.

3 rainbow trout, about 12 oz (340 g) each
juice of 3 lemons
6 tablespoons walnut oil
3-4 sprigs fresh thyme
a few fresh chives
2 oz (60 g) button mushrooms
1 lettuce heart
salt and freshly ground pepper

Ask your fishmonger to skin and fillet the trout. Remove any remaining bones
that you come across. Place the fillets in a shallow dish, and pour over the juice
from the lemons and the walnut oil. Sprinkle with half the thyme and fresh
chives, reserving the remainder for garnish. Leave to marinate for 8 hours,
turning over the fillets about 2 or 3 times during that time.

Meanwhile, wipe the mushrooms clean and cut them lengthways into thin
slices. Wash and dry the lettuce heart. Cut each marinated fillet into three and
arrange the pieces on a serving dish. Garnish with the mushrooms, lettuce
leaves and fresh herbs. Serve.

Serves 6

*Rainbow Trout Salad, Spinach and Chicken
Salad Chinese Style, Glazed Cucumber*

JAMBON PERSILLADE

Use an old-fashioned earthenware crock or an oblong pâté dish for making this parsleyed ham. It goes well with Green Pancakes with Ricotta, p14.

2½-3 lb (1¼-1½ kg) leg of ham or gammon,
most of the fat trimmed off
a large veal bone, chopped into pieces
1 calf's foot
a few sprigs each of tarragon, thyme, parsley, sage
1 bay leaf
1 teaspoon black peppercorns
2 allspice berries (Jamaican peppercorns)
about 1 bottle dry white wine
2 teaspoons white wine vinegar
2 packets (1 tablespoon) gelatine
1 large bunch flat-leaved parsley

Fill a ham kettle or a large pan with cold water. Add the ham and bring slowly to a boil. This operation draws off excess salt. Pour off the water, if it is very salty, and repeat the process again. When the third lot of water is boiling, reduce the heat and simmer for 45 minutes. Remove from the water and cut the meat into chunks. Put the ham back into the rinse-out pan, with the veal bone pieces, calf's foot and, tied in a muslin bag, the tarragon, thyme, parsley, sage, bay leaf, peppercorns and allspice berries. Cover with white wine and bring gently to a boil, skimming the fat from time to time. Cook thoroughly, for about 2 hours.

Dissolve the gelatine in a little of the stock. To make the jelly, strain the stock through a muslin or a fine cloth. Stir in the vinegar and dissolved gelatine and leave to set a little. Finely chop the parsley.

In a bowl, mash the ham. Stir the chopped parsley into the partly set aspic, and add to the ham. Pour into an enamelled, earthenware or china container, about 3 in (7.5 cm) deep, 8 in (20 cm) long and 4 in (10 cm) wide. Set overnight in a refrigerator. Turn out and serve.

Makes 16 slices

Jambon Persillade, Green Pancakes with Ricotta

POUSSINS WITH KUMQUATS

A kumquat is an oval-shaped, small citrus fruit, about 1 in (2.5 cm) long with an edible skin. Kumquats are juicy and tart and go well with poussins. Clementines or tangerines could be substituted for the kumquats. Serve with Egg and Sorrel Cup, p13, and Arab Bread Rolls, p13, which would make an unusual but delectable accompaniment.

4 poussins
4 oz (120 g) butter
8 oz (225 g) kumquats
juice of ½ orange (optional)
1 scant teaspoon arrowroot
salt and freshly ground pepper

Preheat the oven to 475°F/240°C/Gas 9

Fill the 2 halves of a chicken brick with cold water and leave to soak for about 10 minutes. The porous clay will absorb the water which will be converted into steam during cooking, preventing the poussins getting too dry.

Season the poussins, inside and out. Place a little knob of butter in the cavity of each bird, and spread the remaining butter all over the outsides.

Line the bottom half of the brick with foil. Slice 4 kumquats and place them in the bottom. Add the poussins and cover with the other half of the brick. Put in the oven and cook for about 40 to 45 minutes.

Transfer the poussins to a serving dish and keep warm in the switched-off oven while you prepare the sauce. Carefully lift the foil, which will have collected the kumquat-flavoured poussin juice. Discard any pips and blend the juice and cooked kumquat slices in a blender. If the sauce is too thick, add the orange juice. Transfer to a small saucepan and heat. Remove from the heat and, taking one tablespoon of the sauce, blend it in a cup with the arrowroot. Pour the arrowroot mixture back into the sauce and reheat, but do not boil, for a minute or two. Pour the glazed sauce over the poussins. Garnish with the remaining kumquats, sliced. Serve immediately.

Serves 4

Meat and Poultry

SPINACH AND CHICKEN SALAD CHINESE STYLE

I buy young spinach leaves for this salad, as they are more
tender than older leaves. The salad will keep for two days
if refrigerated. Serve with Rainbow Trout Salad, p18,
and Glazed Cucumber, p27.

2 chicken breasts
1 garlic clove
1½ lb (675 g) young spinach leaves
2 tablespoons sunflower oil
1 tablespoon sesame oil
juice of ½ lemon
1 teaspoon soya sauce
1 in (2.5 cm) piece fresh ginger, finely chopped
1 oz (30 g) sesame seeds, lightly toasted

Preheat the oven to 450°F/230°C/Gas 8
Wrap the two chicken breasts with the garlic clove, (unpeeled but cut in two),
in foil and close tightly. Bake for 10 to 15 minutes. Unwrap, discard the garlic
and leave to cool.

Remove the stalks from the spinach, and wash in several changes of
water until scrupulously clean. Shake off the excess water, but do not
dry. Heat one tablespoon of sunflower oil in a large pan. Add in the
spinach pushing it down with a wooden spoon. Reduce the heat, cover and
simmer for 4 to 5 minutes. Remove the lid, give a stir with a spoon (at this stage
the leaves will have reduced quite a lot). Cover and let cook for another 4 to 5
minutes. Transfer to a serving dish, placing each leaf in a loose curl. Pull the
cooked chicken into strands, and add to the spinach.

To prepare the dressing, mix the remaining sunflower oil, sesame oil,
lemon juice, soya sauce and finely chopped fresh ginger root. Pour the dressing
into the salad and toss lightly to evenly coat the spinach and chicken. Sprinkle
the sesame seeds all over; the tiny seeds will adhere to the coated leaves and
strands of chicken.

Serves 2-3

Meat and Poultry

STIR-FRIED BEEF WITH VEGETABLES

Ideally the beef should be stir-fried in a wok over fierce heat, but a straight-sided sauté pan will do. I find a Chinese metal spatula useful for quickly tossing a large quantity of food. This method of cooking seals the food outside, keeping the inside moist, and brings out the colour of the vegetables. Tinned water chestnuts and whole baby corns are available from Chinese supermarkets. Serve with Yoghurt and Courgette Sauce, p32.

2 garlic cloves, finely chopped
1 tablespoon soya sauce
8 oz (225 g) lean beef
1 teaspoon sherry
1 broccoli spear
1 large carrot
1 generous tablespoon olive oil
1 in (2.5 cm) piece fresh ginger root,
finely shredded
6 water chestnuts, quartered
6 whole baby corns
salt

Using a very sharp knife, cut the beef in thin, finger-length strips. Add the soya sauce, garlic and sherry. Toss thoroughly and reserve.

Chop the broccoli into small pieces keeping the florets intact. Peel the carrot, and with a vegetable peeler, cut it, lengthways, in long strands.

In a wok or sauté pan, heat half the oil. When it starts sizzling, add a little salt and swirl it around. Add the beef and, tossing constantly, stir-fry until it begins to brown. Remove from the pan and place on a serving dish. Keep hot.

Heat the remaining oil and add, all at once, the broccoli, carrot, ginger root, water chestnuts and baby corns, cut in two, lengthways, if large. Stir-fry, tossing for a minute or two. Add some salt and transfer to the dish with the beef. Lightly toss the meat and vegetables and serve at once.

Serves 2-3

Stir-Fried Beef with Vegetables, Yoghurt
and Courgette Sauce

PALIA E FIENO SALAD

The literal translation of 'Palia e fieno' is straw and hay,
appropriate for this mixture of yellow and green pasta.
The salad may be made with differently shaped pasta;
there are the spiral-shaped 'fusilli', the butterfly-shaped
'farfalle' and so on. Indeed the choice is endless in
specialised shops, but for this recipe use yellow and green
pasta. The mange-touts are left uncooked, and give a
crunchy texture to the salad. With Scrambled Eggs aux
Deux Verdures, p10, it makes a lovely light lunch.

8 oz (225 g) fresh egg pasta
8 oz (225 g) fresh spinach pasta
8 oz (225 g) cottage cheese
2 tablespoons olive oil
4 oz (120 g) cooked red kidney beans
2 tablespoons cooked kidney beans,
drained and rinsed
8 oz (225 g) mange-touts
1 small bunch fresh coriander
2 tablespoons pine-nuts, lightly toasted
salt and freshly ground pepper

Have ready a large pan of salted boiling water and cook the yellow and green
pasta for about 45 seconds (or for 10-12 minutes, if dried, according to the
packet instructions. The exact time depends on the shape that you have
chosen; fusilli for example would take a few seconds longer. Drain in a
colander and transfer to a bowl. Mix the cottage cheese and olive oil together
and add to the pasta. Toss lightly until evenly distributed.

Add the drained and rinsed red kidney beans to the pasta. Top and tail the
mange-touts. (If the mange-touts are a little wilted, soak them in ice-cold water
for 15 minutes before using.) Tuck the mange-tout decoratively in the salad
and season with salt and freshly ground pepper. Add the lightly toasted
pine-nuts.

Wash and dry the fresh coriander, and use whole leaves as a garnish round
the edge of the dish.

Serves 6

GLAZED CUCUMBER

Here cucumbers are lightly pickled in vinegar, then glazed
with butter and sugar. The pieces are shaped like large
olives and their translucent green combined with the
similar hues of the lime's flesh and rind looks very pretty
indeed. Serve with Rainbow Trout Salad, p18, and
Spinach and Chicken Salad Chinese Style, p23.

2 cucumbers
1 pt (550 ml) cider vinegar
2 oz (60 g) butter
1 tablespoon sugar
salt and freshly ground pepper
1 lime

Peel the cucumbers (I often use a ridged vegetable peeler which 'stripes' the
skin) and cut in 2 in (5 cm) slices. Divide again in three lengthways, and using a
small knife, fashion the pieces into the shape of large olives.

Bring the vinegar to a boil in an enamelled saucepan. Add the cucumber
pieces and cook for 2-3 minutes. Drain.

Melt the butter in a pan and sauté the drained cucumber for 3 minutes.
Sprinkle with the sugar and cook for a further 3 minutes. Season with salt and
freshly ground pepper. Transfer to a shallow dish and garnish with thin slices
of lime, then serve.

Serves 4-6

TOMATOES WITH BURGHUL

'Burghul' is roasted, cracked wheat which is often used in Middle-Eastern cuisine. It is available in three sizes, but I like medium- and coarse-grain burghul which are pleasantly chewy. Burghul can be bought from health food shops or Greek grocers. Serve this dish with Mange-tout Bites, p31, and Tomato and Lime Mayonnaise, p32.

12 tomatoes, medium size
4 oz (120 g) burghul, washed under running water
juice of 2 lemons
1 tablespoon fruity olive oil
a handful fresh mint leaves, chopped
sprigs of mixed herbs
salt and freshly ground pepper

Cut off and reserve a 'hat' from each tomato and using a little spoon, scoop out most of the flesh and all the seeds. Place the tomatoes upside-down on kitchen paper, to drain.

Place the burghul in a large bowl and cover with very lightly salted water. Leave for 15 minutes. By then the burghul should have swollen and absorbed all the water. Drain and squeeze dry in a clean tea-towel. Place the burghul in a bowl with the lemon juice, salt and pepper and leave for about 1 hour.

The burghul is ready when it is chewy but not hard in the centre. (If it is still hard leave for a little longer with more lemon juice.) Add the olive oil and fresh mint, and stir thoroughly. Fill each of the hollowed tomatoes with some of the mixture and top with their reserved hats, if wished. Place sprigs of mixed herbs in a small bowl in the centre of a flat serving dish and surround with the tomatoes. Surround the dish with more mint and serve.

Serves 6-12

Tomatoes with Burghul, Mange-tout Bites,
Tomato and Lime Mayonnaise, Elderflower
Bread, Rocket and Cauliflower Salad

ROCKET AND CAULIFLOWER SALAD

Rocket (*Eruca sativa*) is a salad plant with a sharp,
peppery taste. It is commonly grown in Italy, but
neglected in England. Its flowers are also edible and add a
pretty, spring touch. This salad is nice with Elderflower
Bread, p.15. Watercress can be substituted for the rocket.

1 bunch rocket
2 lettuce hearts
1 small cauliflower
1 teaspoon strong Dijon mustard
juice of 1/2 lemon
3 tablespoons hazelnut oil
salt and freshly ground pepper

Trim most of the rocket leaf stalks. Clean the rocket, reserving the flowers,
and the lettuce hearts and drain. Dry thoroughly.

Cut the cauliflower into florets, and steam for 6-7 minutes. Rinse under cold
running water.

In a small bowl, beat the mustard and lemon juice, using a fork; gradually
add the hazelnut oil to emulsify the dressing. Season with salt and pepper.

In a shallow salad bowl, place the rocket in an outer ring. Make a circle in the
centre with the lettuce leaves, and place the cauliflower florets among the
greens. Pour the dressing over the lettuce and cauliflower only, garnish
with the reserved rocket flowers and serve.

Serves 6-8

MANGE-TOUT BITES

Here the mange-touts are filled with cream cheese
but this may be replaced with Boursault or Brillat-Savarin,
(if so, omit the other ingredients). I prefer medium-size
mange-touts which are less fiddly to deal with than the
very small ones. The purple chive flowers look most
attractive against the bright green mange-touts. Serve the
stuffed mange-touts on their own, or with Tomato and
Lime Mayonnaise; p32, and Tomatoes with
Burghul, p.29.

8 oz (225 g) mange-touts, medium size
4 oz (120 g) cream cheese
1 teaspoon strained horseradish sauce or French mustard
1 teaspoon green peppercorns, lightly crushed (optional)
salt
chive flowers, to garnish

Soak the mange-touts for about 20 minutes in cold water. Snap the stem end
only and pull the string away. Steam for 30 seconds, (unless you prefer
crunchier, raw mange-touts), and rinse swiftly under cold running water.
Shake the colander while rinsing to ensure even cooling and to preserve the
mange-touts' bright colour. Drain.

In a small bowl, mash the cream cheese and horseradish (or French
mustard). The horseradish sauce must be strained or 'bits' get stuck in the
piping nozzle. Season with salt, then transfer to a piping bag fitted with a
small-tipped pastry nozzle. Pipe a little of the creamy mixture inside each
mange-tout, sprinkle with crushed peppercorns, if wished, and garnish with
chive flowers.

Serves 6

Sauces

TOMATO AND LIME MAYONNAISE

Serve with Tomatoes with Burghul, p29, and Mange-
tout Bites, p3, or with cold fish or eggs.

2 egg yolks
10 fl oz (280 ml) walnut or olive oil
1 teaspoon oregano or marjoram
1 tablespoon tomato paste
juice of 1 lime
salt and freshly ground pepper

Bring the eggs and oil up to room temperature before starting.

In a small bowl, beat the yolks with the oregano or marjoram. Still beating, add the walnut oil drop by drop to start with, then in a thin stream. When the mixture starts to emulsify, pour the oil less slowly. Add the tomato paste and lime juice, stirring well to blend all the ingredients. Season to taste with salt and pepper. Cover until needed.

Makes 12 fl oz (340 ml)

YOGHURT AND COURGETTE SAUCE

This is a sauce to serve with Stir-fried Beef with
Vegetables, p24, with pasta, or with an egg dish.

8 oz (225 g) courgettes
2 teaspoons fruity olive oil
10 fl oz (280 ml) yoghurt
5 fl oz (150 ml) sour cream
1 tablespoon fresh thyme
salt and freshly ground pepper
a few rosemary flowers (optional)

Top and tail the courgettes. Clean them and pat dry. Chop into small pieces. Heat the oil in a pan and sauté the courgettes over high heat, tossing constantly with a wooden spoon, for about 2 minutes.

In a small bowl, beat together the yoghurt and sour cream. Add the thyme, crushing it to allow its fragrance to escape. Season to taste, toss in the courgettes, garnish with the rosemary flowers, if using, and serve.

Makes 1 pt (550 ml)

SABAYON SAUCE

This sauce is lovely with Frozen Creamed Rice, p37. To transform this sauce into a frozen sabayon mousse, add the stiffly beaten whites of the eggs to the cooled sauce. Pour into a soufflé dish or individual goblets and freeze. Serve with Brittle Lime Biscuits, p39.

4 egg yolks
2 oz (60 g) sugar
5 fl oz (150 ml) Marsala,
or other fortified wine

In the top part of a double boiler, or a large mixing bowl placed over a pan of simmering water, whip the 4 egg yolks and sugar until the mixture becomes pale yellow and creamy. Add the marsala, or other fortified wine, and continue beating until thick and foamy. The sauce is ready when it forms soft peaks. Transfer to a jug and serve at once.

PRALINÉ CREAM

This is a rich pudding which is served semi-frozen. It has
a smooth texture with crunchy praliné bits inside.

2 oz (60 g) granulated sugar
2 oz (60 g) hazelnuts, finely chopped
oil for greasing
10 fl oz (280 ml) whipping cream, chilled
2 tablespoons castor sugar
2 tablespoons Drambuie
6 oz (170 g) marzipan
crystallized angelica (optional)

In a heavy pan, melt the granulated sugar until it turns a light brown. Stir in the nuts and pour onto a greased surface. Allow to cool and solidify, then break the praliné into small pieces or process quickly in a food processor.

Whip the chilled cream with the sugar and Drambuie. Chop the marzipan in the food processor until reduced to small bits. In a bowl, mix the praliné and marzipan. Fold into the cream mixture. Pour into 6 to 8 goblets and freeze from 1½ to 3 hours. Decorate each goblet with matchstick-sized strips of angelica, if desired, then serve.

Serves 6-8

Praliné Cream, Purple Honey, Lemon Curd
Ice Cream, Rose-Geranium Sorbet

Desserts

ROSE-GERANIUM SORBET

This sorbet is scented with leaves from the rose-geranium.
The flavour is subtle with a delicate fragrance, and the
sorbet should be eaten very fresh. You can substitute 1
tablespoon of rose-water for the rose geranium leaves.

10 rose-geranium leaves,
plus extra for decoration
4 oz (120 g) sugar
juice of 1 lemon
1 egg white, stiffly beaten

Steep 10 rose-geranium leaves in 1 pt (550 ml) of boiling water. Leave for
about 1 hour. Boil the sugar in 5 fl oz (150 ml) water for a minute or two. Cool.
In a bowl, strain the rose-geranium flavoured water into the syrup, stir in the
lemon juice and freeze.

When the mixture begins to set, beat it vigorously to break up the ice
crystals, and fold in the stiffly beaten egg white. Freeze again. Half an hour
before serving, transfer to the refrigerator and allow the sorbet to soften
slightly. Eat the same day, decorated at the very last moment with rose-
geranium leaves.

Serves 6

PURPLE HONEY

This honey is coloured with the tiny purple-blue seeds of
the poppy. It is nice spread on toast or as a filling for a pie.

8 fl oz (225 ml) light honey
6 oz (170 g) poppy seeds
about 2 heaped tablespoons currants (optional)

In a heavy saucepan, melt together the honey, 2 tablespoons water, poppy
seeds and currants, if used. Cook gently stirring constantly, for about 15
minutes, or until thick. Pot and cover.

Makes 15 fl oz (420 ml)

Desserts

LEMON CURD ICE CREAM

This is a quickly made recipe which is done in a matter of
minutes. Its bright yellow colour would go well with a few
green mint leaves.

1 lb (450 g) pot lemon curd
1 pint (550 ml) plain yoghurt
rind of 1 lemon, cut into thin strips
a few mint leaves (optional)

In a mixing bowl, thoroughly combine the lemon curd and yoghurt. Pour into
a metal bowl or ice tray and freeze for at least 5 hours. This ice cream needs no
additional beating part-way through the freezing process.
   Serve scooped out into individual glass cups (previously left in the freezer
for an hour or so – they will be frosted when brought to the table). Or present
the ice cream sliced, like cake, on an oblong dish. In either case decorate with
thin strips of lemon rind, and mint leaves, if used.

Serves 8

◆

FROZEN CREAMED RICE

Here the rice gives an interesting texture to this frozen
pudding, not unlike 'kulfi' (Indian ice cream). It is
delicious with Brittle Lime Biscuits, p39, fresh pineapple
or red fruits. Serve with Sabayon Sauce, p33, for a special treat.

3 oz (90 g) pudding rice
1 pt (550 ml) rich milk
1 vanilla pod, split open
2-3 tablespoons castor sugar
5 fl oz (150 ml) whipping cream

This is best made in a double boiler. Place the rice, milk and vanilla pod in the
top pan, cover and simmer for about 1½ hours, stirring from time to time and
replenishing the water in the bottom pan, if necessary. Once the rice has
absorbed all the milk and looks like a creamy mush speckled with tiny particles
from the vanilla pod, stir in the castor sugar and leave to cool. Refrigerate until
chilled, remove the vanilla pod, then fold in the whipped cream and freeze.

Serves 4-6

Desserts and Drinks

BRITTLE LIME BISCUITS

Serve these delicious biscuits with Frozen Creamed Rice,
p37 or Sabayon Sauce, p33, and Batida de Café.

4 oz (120 g) plain flour
4 oz (120 g) rice flour
3 oz (85 g) castor sugar
3 oz (85 g) butter, chilled and cubed
zest of 1 lime, finely chopped
1 egg yolk
oil for greasing
sugar for sprinkling

Preheat the oven to 350°F/180°C/Gas 4
   Mix the flour, rice flour and sugar. Rub in the butter and add the lime zest.
Mix the egg yolk with a little water and add it to the other ingredients to make a
smooth dough. Roll out thinly and cut into heart shapes.
   Place on greased greaseproof paper and bake for 12 minutes. Sprinkle with a
little sugar and lift off carefully. Cool the brittle biscuits on a wire rack. They
will keep well in an airtight jar or tin.

Makes about 2 dozen biscuits

BATIDA DE CAFÉ

'Batida' is a Brazilian cocktail. The word 'batida' means
beaten or whipped. Serve with Brittle Lime Biscuits and
Frozen Creamed Rice, p37, and Sabayon Sauce, p33.

2 fl oz (60 ml) dark rum
1 tablespoon dark cane sugar
10 fl oz (280 ml) very strong coffee
1 egg white
crushed ice

Mix all the ingredients and blend in a blender for a few seconds. Pour into 2 tall
goblets, adding more crushed ice if necessary, and serve.

Serves 2

Batida de Café, Sabayon Sauce, Brittle Lime Biscuits, Frozen Creamed Rice

SUMMER

Summer should be a pleasurable season for those who prepare meals as well as for those who consume them. More often than not, the 'cook' has other eminently visible and demanding roles to play: that of host or hostess at social occasions; that of parent or spouse at family meals, perhaps even all roles – including cook – at once. Meals or menus that demand excessive amounts of time or finicky, last-minute preparation, have no place in the summer months. Being trapped in a kitchen, especially if it is hot and sunny outdoors, is something to be avoided at all costs.

Summer days are salad days: exquisite combinations of fresh vegetables, chosen as much for their appearance as for their taste; vegetables or fruit and thin slices or slivers of fish, meat or poultry; local soft fruits and more exotic fruits to end a meal. In very hot weather, I use meat, poultry and fish with restraint, to add spark to a dish, or even as a garnish, rather than as traditional, obligatory and stodgy protein. Appetites and palates can become jaded in hot weather but smaller portions of carefully selected ingredients, presented as a feast for the eyes, are tempting and successful. Delectable, and most well received in the summer months, are jellied dishes, either savoury or sweet, that can be prepared the night before and presented as shimmering *faits accomplis*. Cold soufflés, too, contrast and complement the simplicity of salads without demanding enormous amounts of last-minute attention.

Farther afield, summer is a time for moveable feasts, for meals that can be packed up and taken to a picnic a few minutes or a few hours away, that look as presentable when unwrapped or decanted as when first made. Home-made fruit curds, a pâté of black olives and a fresh tomato 'cheese' are welcome additions to picnic fare and, with fresh bread, seem to expand to accommodate unexpected guests and increased appetites. Home-made fruit juices provide a light and cleansing end to a summer meal, but are equally well received on their own, as refreshing mid-morning or mid-afternoon drinks, or at the close of a perfect summer's day.

CHIVES BOULETTES

First a word about the chives: you may be able to find what the French call 'ciboule', which is a giant chive, about half an inch (1.5 cm) in diameter. If so, it would be a good idea to use a mixture of the two sorts of chives. If not, chop the normal chives in two sizes, fine and coarse. Either way, you will achieve a pretty effect.

Serve this dish on its own as an appetizer, or to accompany courgette flowers in Vietnamese Batter, p44.

8 oz (225 g) cream or curd cheese
4 oz (120 g) mixed grated cheeses*
3 tablespoons olive or hazelnut oil
5 tablespoons fresh chives, chopped
2 heads red chicory (radicchio)

With a large fork, mash until smooth the cream or curd cheese – a task made easier if the cheese is at room temperature. Add the grated cheeses mixture and the olive or hazelnut oil.

Shape into small balls, the size of a walnut, rolling each boulette in the chopped chives and placing it in the centre of a red chicory leaf.

*Use a mixture of Parmesan, Wensleydale and Emmental; a mixture of Stilton, Farmhouse Cheddar and Double Gloucester; or any other combination of leftover cheeses.

Makes 2 dozen boulettes

Chives Boulettes, Vietnamese Batter, courgettes

VIETNAMESE BATTER

In this recipe neither milk nor egg yolk is used and the result is a crisp, light batter. The sesame oil imparts an oriental touch to the deep-fried vegetables. I like to make this batter for coating button mushrooms or courgette flowers, the latter stem on, but calyx removed.

2 oz (60 g) cornflour
2 oz (60 g) flour
1 teaspoon dried thyme
a pinch of paprika
a pinch of salt
1/2 teaspoon dried yeast
3 fl oz (85 ml) beer or soda-water
1 dessertspoon sesame oil
1 egg white
oil for frying

Sift together the cornflour, flour, thyme, paprika and salt. Sprinkle the yeast in 3 fl oz (85 ml) warm water and stir to dissolve. Leave for about 10 minutes to bubble and become frothy. Make a well in the flour mixture and add the yeast stirring briskly to avoid lumps forming, and then add the beer (or soda-water) and sesame oil. Beat until the batter is a creamy consistency. A little more liquid may be necessary, depending on the absorption of the flour. Leave to rest in a warm place for 30-60 minutes. Fold in the stiffly beaten egg white just before using.

Heat the oil in a wok or deep pot. Dip a few vegetables or flowers at a time into the batter using a slotted spoon or an oriental mesh dipper, available from oriental cookery supply stores. Transfer the coated vegetables or flowers to the hot oil and fry until golden. (A deep frying basket is useful if you are using a large pot.) Remove and drain on paper towels. Keep warm while you repeat the exercise with the remaining vegetables or flowers, then serve immediately.

**Makes enough batter for 12 oz (350 g) button mushrooms,
or 10 courgette flowers**

Eggs, Cheeses and Grains

Marmoreal Eggs

This recipe is based on the Chinese tea eggs. When
shelled the eggs present an attractive marbled appearance.
I think that either Lapsang Souchong or Oolong tea gives
a nice fragrance to the spicy eggs. Serve with Baked
Lettuce and Radicchio with Hazelnut Sauce, p62, and
Coppa and Endive Boats, p53.

8 eggs
4 tablespoons Chinese tea leaves
2 sticks of cinnamon bark
3-4 star anise or $\frac{1}{2}$ teaspoon aniseed
1 piece dried orange peel
2 tablespoons soya sauce
1 teaspoon salt

Place the eggs in a saucepan and cover with water. Bring to the boil and cook for
10 minutes. Remove the eggs and, very gently, evenly crack the shells with the
back of a large, heavy spoon.

Return the eggs to the pan and cover with plenty of water. Add the tea
leaves, cinnamon bark, star anise (or aniseed), orange peel, soya sauce and salt.
Bring to a boil and cook gently for about 2 hours, replenishing the water if
necessary. Leave to cool and soak for a few hours in the spicy tea. Shell
carefully, then serve.

Serves 4-8

SMOKED HADDOCK AND COURGETTE SALAD

Translucent, paper-thin slices of smoked haddock make
an unusual alternative to smoked salmon.
Try serving the salad with Rillettes D'Olive p68, and
Broccoli with Coconut Milk, p56.

2 or 3 baby courgettes, preferably
a mixture of yellow and green ones
smoked haddock fillet, about 12 oz (340 g)
2-3 tablespoons olive oil
a few sprigs of fresh basil
a few pink peppercorns,
lightly crushed (optional)
salt and freshly ground pepper

Slice, but don't peel, the courgettes. Place them in a bamboo steaming basket, season with salt and pepper and cover with the lid. (The basil stems, leaves reserved, may be placed in the pan to flavour the vegetable.) Steam for 2-3 minutes and refresh under cold water, then drain. (As a matter of taste, baby courgettes are delicious eaten raw.)

The haddock is used raw and, as it is important to cut it paper-thin, I prefer to freeze it first. That way it is much easier to shave off slivers, using a sharp knife and discarding any bone encountered. You will be left with the skin which is thrown away.

To assemble, have ready a round, flat serving dish and, as you cut the fish, place the slices in overlapping circles on the dish. Garnish the centre with the cooled courgettes, making a nice pattern. Lightly brush the fish with olive oil, then pour the oil in a thin stream over the courgettes, seasoning the latter again with salt and pepper. Tear the basil leaves over the salad (they lose their pungency if cut), sprinkle with pink peppercorns, if using, and serve.

Serves 6

Smoked Haddock and Courgette Salad, Broccoli with Coconut Milk,
Rillettes d'Olive, Quick Fromage Blanc

SALMON AND TROUT PARCELS

This dish goes well with crunchy salads, such as Yellow and Green Courgette Salad, p66, and Tomato and Carrot Salad, p66, which counterbalance the smoothness and rich taste of the parcels.

2 smoked trout
6 smoked salmon slices
2-3 tablespoons sour cream
1 teaspoon horseradish
1 teaspoon lemon juice
small bunch of fresh dill
1 lemon
freshly ground pepper

Remove the flesh from the smoked trout, discarding any bone. Place the flesh into a small bowl, mash it with the sour cream, then add the horseradish and lemon juice. Season with one or two turns of the pepper mill. Take half of the dill, cut it with scissors over the smoked trout and stir to blend.

Lay one smoked salmon slice (cut in half if they are very large), on a flat surface. At one end place a little of the trout mixture and roll it up. Place a dill sprig on each parcel and place on a serving dish. Repeat the operation with the remaining salmon and garnish with thin slices of lemon. Cover and refrigerate until needed.

Serves 8

Salmon and Trout Parcels, Yellow and Green Courgette Salad, Tomato and Carrot Salad

CHICKEN WITH MUSTARD SEEDS AND FRESH PASTA

You can use the recipe for Speckled Ribbons, p124, instead of buying tagliatelle. Half an hour before the chicken is ready, prepare the pasta and sauce. Serve with French Bean and Mushroom Salad, p57, and Mustard and Tarragon Sauce, p69.

1 chicken, preferably corn fed
3 teaspoons black mustard seeds
3 garlic cloves, peeled
pinch of coarse sea salt
4 oz (120 g) butter
5 fl oz (150 ml) white wine or chicken stock
1½ lb (675 g) fresh spinach tagliatelle
salt and freshly ground pepper
1 teaspoon poppy seeds

For the sauce
5 purple garlic cloves, peeled
1 scant tablespoon black mustard seeds
5 fl oz (150 ml) double cream
2 egg yolks

In a mortar, crush 2 teaspoons of mustard seeds, the garlic and salt. Rub the mixture over the chicken and marinate, refrigerated, for 12 hours.

Heat half of the butter in a heavy saucepan, and sauté the chicken until browned. Cook uncovered until cooked, about 1¼ hours, adding the wine (or stock) at frequent intervals. To prepare the sauce, blanch the peeled garlic cloves for 5 minutes. Drain. Crush the mustard seeds in a mortar. Blend the garlic, mustard seeds, cream and egg yolks. Season, then place the mixture in a bowl over a pan of gently boiling water, and stir until the sauce has thickened and coats the back of a spoon. Whisk thoroughly. Cook the tagliatelle for 45 seconds in boiling salted water. Drain and toss the pasta in the remaining butter. Reserve.

Joint the chicken. Make a bed of tagliatelle and place the chicken on top. Scatter over the remaining mustard seeds and the poppy seeds. Serve accompanied by the sauce.

Serves 4

Chicken with Mustard Seeds and Fresh Pasta, French Bean and Mushroom Salad, Mustard and Tarragon Sauce

VEAL AND ORANGE RING

This jewel-like jellied ring goes very well with deep green
Gâteau de Fenouil, page 61, Baked Avocado with Eggs,
p58, and Avocado Sauce, p67. For a special 'party
presentation', add blanched julienne strips of orange rind
to the triangles of veal and fresh orange segments.

1 tablespoon oil
1 lb (450 g) piece leg of veal
2 tablespoons Cognac
4 oranges
1 lemon
2 tablespoons Grand Marnier
1 tablespoon white wine vinegar
1 pt (550 ml) stock, clarified
1 packet (1/2 tablespoon) gelatine
salt and freshly ground pepper
nasturtium flowers and leaves, to garnish

Preheat the oven to 350°F/180°C/Gas 4
Heat the oil in a small, heavy roasting pan and brown the veal. When it is
golden, pour in the Cognac and flame. Roast the veal for 30-40 minutes; it
should still be pink in the centre. Transfer to a plate and leave to cool.

Prepare the sauce in the roasting tin. Add to the meat juices, the juice of 2
oranges and the lemon, the Grand Marnier, vinegar and stock. Bring to the
boil, stirring, then strain and leave to cool. Meanwhile, soften the gelatine in
about 2 tablespoons of warm water, then add it to the sauce, together with salt
and pepper, stirring until the gelatine is totally dissolved. Peel the 2 remaining
oranges, removing the pith, pips and membranes. Cut the veal into thin slices
and then into small triangles.

Chill a 1½ pt (840 ml) savarin mould in the freezer for 5-10 minutes, then
line the bottom and sides of the ring with a little of the jelly; it should set at once.
Arrange the veal pieces and orange sections in the bottom of the mould. Dip
each piece in jelly first, to help it remain in the right position. Add just enough
jelly to cover the veal and orange segments, then chill. Set each layer before
arranging the next, gently warming the remaining jelly if it starts to set. Once
the mould is full, refrigerate for at least 4 hours.

Unmould the ring onto a round serving dish, then garnish with nasturtium
flowers in the centre, and nasturtium leaves and flowers round the edge.

Serves 8

COPPA AND ENDIVE BOATS

'Coppa' is a cured shoulder of pork and is a speciality of
the province of Parma in Italy. Coppa is the size of a very
large sausage and is best eaten cut in paper-thin slices.
Proscuitto can be substituted for the coppa. These little
coppa- and cheese-filled boats go well with Marmoreal
Eggs, p45, and Baked Lettuce and Radicchio with
Hazelnut Sauce, p62.

4 oz (120 g) coppa, cut in very thin slices
8 oz (325 g) ricotta cheese
2-3 sage leaves, finely chopped
coarsely ground black peppercorns
2-3 medium-size Belgian endive
walnut oil

Lay 4 coppa slices flat on a wooden board. Cut off a slice of ricotta cheese and
cut it again to make 4 narrow, long pieces, each more or less the length of a
coppa slice. Sprinkle a little sage and pepper over the coppa, then roll them
around the ricotta and place on a plate. Repeat the operation with the
remaining ingredients, doing four at a time. Lightly brush walnut oil over the
rolls to keep them moist and shiny.

Place the Belgian endive, separated into leaves, on a serving dish, making an
outer and then an inner circle. Fill each leaf with a coppa parcel, and serve.

This recipe makes about 20 boats

*Potages de Fanes en Gelée, Cucumber
and Mint Savarin, curled
cucumber strips*

Vegetables and Salads

POTAGE DE FANES EN GELÉE

This is a very old-fashioned recipe. 'Fanes' here is the
French word for radish leaves, which are peppery and give
a sharp tangy flavour to this jellied soup. The soup is
garnished with long omelette strands. It is a good soup to
serve with a rich dish, such as Salmon and Trout Parcels,
p48. This soup may be served hot, but then omit the
gelatine. The remaining radishes may be used for a salad
with prawns, accompanied by Mustard and Tarragon
Sauce, p69.

3-4 radish bunches
1½ pt (840 ml) vegetable or chicken stock
salt and freshly ground black pepper
1 packet (½ tablespoon) gelatine
1 oz (30 g) butter
2 eggs
3 tablespoons parsley, finely chopped
a pinch of mace

Cut off the leaves from the radishes, (reserving a few of them for garnish).
Wash and dry the leaves, then chop roughly. Put the leaves in a heavy enamel
saucepan, add the stock and salt and pepper, according to taste. Bring
the mixture to the boil, then reduce the heat and simmer for 20 minutes.
Take a cupful of very hot stock and sprinkle in the gelatine, stirring briskly for a
minute or two to dissolve it.

Blend the leaves and stock in a blender, then add the strained gelatine/stock
mixture. Transfer to a bowl, cool, then chill for several hours.

Make a very thin omelette in the usual way with the butter, eggs and parsley,
seasoning with mace, salt and pepper. When cooked, transfer it to a large
wooden board and let cool for 5 minutes or so. With a sharp knife, cut the
omelette into long, thin strands. Keep in foil until needed.

To serve, transfer the jellied soup, which should be set, but not too firm,
into a soup tureen. Garnish the soup with omelette strands and very thinly
sliced radishes.

Serves 6

Vegetables and Salads

BROCCOLI WITH COCONUT MILK

Serve with Smoked Haddock and Courgette Salad, p46.

1½ lb (675 g) broccoli, trimmed
8 oz (225 g) packet creamed coconut
10 fl oz (280 ml) milk
1 tablespoon black mustard seeds
1 teaspoon caraway seeds
2-3 oz (60-85 g) cooked red kidney beans, drained and rinsed
salt and freshly ground pepper

Steam the broccoli for about 7-10 minutes. Rinse under cold running water. Reserve. Heat the coconut and milk, stirring constantly until the coconut has dissolved. Remove from the heat. Add the mustard and caraway seeds, reserving a few. Season, then add the broccoli. Transfer to a serving dish, then garnish with kidney beans, and the reserved seeds.

Serves 4-6

CUCUMBER AND MINT SAVARIN

Serve with Tomato, and Carrot Salads, p66.

8 oz (225 g) cream cheese
5 fl oz (150 ml) sour cream or creamed smatana
5 fl oz (150 ml) chicken stock
1 packet (½ tablespoon) gelatine
1 large cucumber
juice of ½ lemon
5-6 sprigs fresh mint
salt and white pepper

Beat the cream cheese and sour cream (or smatana) until smooth. Heat the stock, then sprinkle the gelatine over the stock. Stir until dissolved. Reserve. Peel the cucumber, reserving the peel; chop the flesh finely and add to the cheese. Add the lemon juice, then season. Strain the stock into the mixture and stir. Add half of the mint leaves, finely chopped. Pour into a rinsed, but not dried, 8 in (20 cm) savarin mould, and chill. Before serving, invert the savarin onto a dish. Garnish with mint leaves and cucumber peel.

Serves 6-8

GREEN TOMATO AND BLACK PLUM SALAD

Serve with Cold Aubergine Soufflé, p60, Basil and Raw
tomato Sauce, p69, and Banana and Gruyère Salad, p65.

1 lb (450 g) small green tomatoes
1 lb (450 g) dark plums, stoned
2-3 drops Worcestershire sauce
4 tablespoons olive oil
juice of 1 lime, zest removed
and sliced into thin strips
1 teaspoon coriander seeds,
powdered in a mortar
salt and 1 teaspoon crushed green peppercorns

Slice the tomatoes into thin wedges. Slice the plums. Mix the Worcestershire
sauce, olive oil, lime juice and coriander seeds. Season and toss the tomatoes
and plums in the dressing. Garnish with lime curls and peppercorns.

Serves 4

FRENCH BEAN AND MUSHROOM SALAD

Serve with Chicken with Mustard Seeds and French
Pasta, p50 and Mustard and Tarragon Sauce, p69.

1 lb (450 g) small French beans
5 Parma ham slices
8 oz (225 g) mushrooms, wiped clean
2 tablespoons hazelnut oil
juice of 1/2 lemon
salt
2 savory sprigs, in flower
1/2 teaspoon peppercorns

Wash and trim the French beans. Steam for 5 to 6 minutes, then rinse under
cold water. Cut the ham slices in 2, lengthways; twist each one, making a
'ribbon'. Divide the beans into 10 equal bundles. Tie each with a ham strand.
Place on a serving dish. Trim the mushroom stalks and cut the mushrooms
lengthways. Arrange the slices between the bundles. Blend the oil, lemon juice
and salt. Pour over the salad and garnish with savory and peppercorns.

Makes 10 bundles

BAKED AVOCADO WITH EGGS

For a variation on the egg and avocado theme, place a soft-boiled egg in each avocado half and serve with the Basil and Raw Tomato Sauce, p.69.

2 very large avocado pears
4 small eggs
dash of paprika
dash of celery salt

Preheat the oven to 350°F/180°C/Gas 4

Cut the avocado pears in two, then remove the stone and break an egg into each cavity. (If the cavity seems too small to hold the egg, scoop out a little of the avocado's flesh.) Season with paprika and celery salt.

Bake directly in a 'bain-marie' for 8 to 10 minutes or until the egg whites are just set. Serve at once.

Serves 4

Partially prepared Baked Avocado with Eggs, Gâteau de Fenouil, Veal and Orange Ring, Avocado Sauce

COLD AUBERGINE SOUFFLÉ

Contrast the richness of the soufflé by serving it with Basil
and Raw Tomato Sauce, p69, and Green Tomato and
Black Plum Salad, p57.

3 oz (85 g) fresh breadcrumbs
5 fl oz (150 ml) milk
3 lb (1.5 kg) aubergines
3 tablespoons fruity olive oil
6 eggs
1 large bunch flat-leaved parsley, chopped
5 fl oz (150 ml) double cream or sour cream
1-2 basil sprigs
oil
salt and freshly ground pepper
a little melted butter

Preheat the oven to 375°F/190°C/Gas 5
Soak the breadcrumbs in the milk. Meanwhile prepare the aubergines. Wash
them and pat dry. Peel the aubergines, reserving a little of the skin for garnish,
and cut the flesh into thin slices. Place in a colander and sprinkle with salt.
Leave for about 15 minutes to disgorge their bitter juice. (This operation also
prevents the aubergines from absorbing too much oil.) Rinse and pat the
aubergines dry, using paper towels. Heat the olive oil in a heavy pan, add the
aubergines, cover and cook gently until softened, about 15 minutes. Chop
them coarsely and reserve.

In a large bowl, beat the eggs, season and add a third of the chopped parsley.
Squeeze the excess milk from the breadcrumbs and incorporate the breadcrumbs into the egg mixture. Add the aubergine and double cream or sour
cream. Mix well and leave for 10 to 15 minutes to allow all flavours to blend.

Line the bottom and sides of a 2 pt (1 litre) charlotte mould or soufflé dish
with non-stick or waxed paper and brush with butter and oil. Pour half the
soufflé mixture into the mould: smooth with a wooden spoon, scatter over the
second third of the parsley and all the basil torn in small pieces. Cover with the
rest of the soufflé mixture. Smooth the surface and bake in a 'bain-marie' for 40
minutes in the oven.

Let cool before unmoulding. Brush the soufflé with oil, then scatter the
remaining chopped parsley on the side. Make a criss-cross pattern on top,
using the reserved aubergine skin, and serve.

Serves 6

GÂTEAU DE FENOUIL

In this recipe, it is important to use very fresh ricotta cheese, as ricotta quickly loses its lovely flavour. For a variation, substitute Swiss chard for the spinach leaves. The 'cake' makes a nice accompaniment for Veal and Orange Ring, p52, and Avocado Sauce, p67.

2 lb (1 kg) fennel bulbs
1 oz (30 g) butter
a pinch of mace
2 sage leaves, very finely chopped
1 lb (450 g) ricotta cheese
2 tablespoons yoghurt or creamed smatana
3 eggs, beaten
2 oz (60 g) freshly grated parmesan cheese
about 8 large spinach leaves
vegetable oil for greasing
2 large carrots
freshly ground pepper

Preheat the oven to 400°F/200°C/Gas 6

Trim and clean the fennel, reserving the feathery leaves for the garnish, and cut the bulb in four. Parboil or steam for 8-10 minutes. Melt the butter in a sauté pan, add the fennel, cover and gently cook for 20 minutes. Add the mace and sage, and process in a food processor.

Beat the ricotta cheese, yoghurt (or creamed smatana), the beaten eggs and the parmesan cheese into the fennel purée. Reserve.

Clean thoroughly, but do not dry the spinach leaves. Steam the leaves for one minute. Refresh under cold water, and pat dry. Grease a 2 pt (1 litre) charlotte mould and line it with the spinach, the stems joining in the centre, the tips upright on the sides of the mould. Pour in the fennel mixture, folding over the overlapping spinach leaves. Bake in a 'bain-marie' in the oven for 45 to 50 minutes. Prick the centre of the mould with a sharp knife blade: it should come out clean. If not, leave the mould in the oven for a few minutes, or until done.

Meanwhile peel and cut the two carrots, lengthways, into thin slices and immerse in a bowl filled with icy water for an hour or so. Drain and reserve.

Take the mould out of the oven, let cool for a few minutes and unmould, inverting the green 'gâteau' onto a serving dish. Surround with the reserved fennel leaves and carrot curls and serve.

Serves 8

BAKED LETTUCE AND RADICCHIO WITH HAZELNUT SAUCE

Red chicory is often called 'radicchio' and has a slightly bitter taste. The dish is a lovely partner for Marmoreal Eggs, p45, and Coppa and Endive Boats, p53.

2 lettuce hearts
2 medium-size red chicory (radicchio)
1 oz (30 g) butter
salt and freshly ground pepper

For the sauce
3 oz (100 g) hazelnuts
4 fl oz (125 ml) sour cream
1 garlic clove, crushed
a pinch of nutmeg
a pinch of cinnamon
salt and freshly ground pepper

Preheat the oven to 350°F/180°C/Gas 4

Cut off the stalks and remove any wilted outer leaves, if necessary, from the green and red salads. Run under cold water until the lettuce heart and red chicory are free from grit and soil. Dry them with a clean tea-towel. Butter the inside of an ovenproof dish which will look pretty on the table, and cut each lettuce heart and red chicory in two. Place them in the dish, cut-side up. Season with salt and freshly ground pepper, and bake for 5 to 6 minutes.

Meanwhile prepare the sauce: toast the hazelnuts under a grill until the skin flakes and the nuts are golden. Rub off the skins and chop the nuts into fairly fine pieces. In a small bowl, mix the sour cream, garlic clove, nutmeg and cinnamon. Season and add the hazelnuts.

When the salads are cooked, spoon over some of the hazelnut sauce. Serve at once, with the rest of the sauce as an accompaniment.

Serves 4

Marmoreal Eggs, Coppa and Endive Boats partially prepared Baked Lettuce and Radicchio with Hazelnut Sauce

BANANA AND GRUYÈRE SALAD

This unusual combination is delicious; the tang of the cheese is balanced by the sweet slightly bland taste of the banana. Serve it with Basil and Raw Tomato Sauce, p69, Green Tomato and Black Plum Salad, p57, and Cold Aubergine Soufflé, p60.

8 oz (225 g) gruyère cheese
2-3 bananas
5 fl oz (150 ml) sour cream
1 tablespoon mayonnaise
1 teaspoon caraway seeds
2-3 sprigs fresh tarragon
salt
white pepper

Cut the gruyère in long, narrow pieces, about the size of a French bean. Peel and slice the bananas. Combine in a bowl and set on one side.

In a small bowl, combine the sour cream, mayonnaise and half of the caraway seeds. Season to your taste with salt and white pepper.

Pour the sauce over the cheese and banana and transfer to a colourful serving dish. Garnish with the whole tarragon leaves and the remaining caraway seeds.

Serves 6

Banana and Gruyère Salad, Cold Aubergine Soufflé, Basil and Raw Tomato Sauce, Green Tomato and Black Plum Salad

Vegetables and Salads

YELLOW AND GREEN COURGETTE SALAD

This is delicious served with Salmon and Trout Parcels, p48.

8 oz (225 g) small green courgettes
8 oz (225 g) small yellow courgettes
3 thyme sprigs
a handful of coconut chips
3 tablespoons hazelnut oil
juice of ¹/₂ lemon
salt freshly ground pepper

Preheat the oven to 400°F/200°C/Gas 6
Trim the courgettes and cut into a mixture of thin strips and circles. Bring some water to the boil with the stripped thyme stalks (reserving the leaves) and steam the courgettes for 2 minutes in a metal or Chinese bamboo steamer. Cool immediately under cold running water, and drain. Spread the coconut chips on an oven tray lined with foil. Dribble over a little of the oil and sprinkle with the thyme leaves; brown in the oven, stirring occasionally for 8 to 10 minutes.

In a shallow salad bowl, lightly toss the courgettes and half the coconut chips. Add the remaining hazelnut oil and the lemon juice, season and toss again. At the last minute scatter the reserved coconut chips on top and serve.

Serves 4-6

TOMATO AND CARROT SALAD

The colour combinations of this salad looks like a Fauvist painting. For a very dramatic effect, use a bright green or yellow dish. I like to serve it with Salmon and Trout Parcels, p48.

1 lb (450 g) small tomatoes
1 lb (450 g) carrots
2 limes
juice of ¹/₂ orange
1 tablespoon fruity olive oil
salt and freshly ground pepper

Clean and wipe dry the tomatoes, and cut into 8 wedges and reserve.

Top and tail the carrots and scrub under cold running water. Dry and chop coarsely, using a heavy knife or a food processor. Place the carrots in a serving dish. Blend together the juice of 1 lime and the orange juice, olive oil, salt and freshly ground pepper. Pour most of dressing over the carrots and toss. Place the tomato wedges and the other lime, thinly sliced, over the carrots. Pour over the remaining dressing and serve immediately.

Serves 4-6

AVOCADO SAUCE

This sauce should be prepared at the last minute, as the avocado's flesh tends to discolour quickly, even with the addition of lime juice. This sauce is nice with Gâteau de Fenouil, p61, a steamed white fish, hard-boiled eggs or on its own with toasted pitta bread.

2 avocado pears, very ripe
juice of 1 lime
2 tablespoons ricotta cheese
2 tablespoons yoghurt or creamed smatana
a few shavings of fresh ginger root
2 tablespoons chopped coriander leaves
cayenne pepper
paprika
salt

Scoop out the avocado flesh and place it into a mixing bowl, adding the lime juice. Mash with a fork until the texture is like that of cottage cheese. Add the ricotta, yoghurt or creamed smatana, ginger shavings, 1 tablespoon of chopped coriander, a dash each of cayenne pepper and paprika, and salt to your taste. Stir all the ingredients thoroughly, then garnish with the remaining coriander leaves.

Makes 7 fl oz (200 ml)

QUICK FROMAGE BLANC

In this recipe, the ricotta gives a slightly grainy texture.
For a richer, smoother and more velvety version, use
instead cream cheese or 'mascarpone', an Italian
equivalent. Quick Fromage Blanc goes well with Tomato
Cheese, p73, Gooseberry Curd, p72, Rillettes d'Olive and
hot toast.

1 lb (450 g) ricotta cheese
5 fl oz (150 ml) single cream or sour cream
5 fl oz (150 ml) natural yoghurt or buttermilk
fresh chives, finely chopped (optional)

In a large bowl, beat all the ingredients until well blended. Refrigerate until
needed. If serving as a savoury, garnish with chopped chives.
    Serve with salt and freshly ground pepper and any fresh herbs available,
chopped into it; or with castor sugar as a pudding.

Serves 6-8

RILLETTES D'OLIVE

This is a dish to serve with Quick Fromage Blanc and hot
toast, or as a sauce with a grilled or poached fish.

6 oz (170 g) black olives, preferably herbed
3 oz (85 g) unsalted butter
1 teaspoon thyme
a pinch of oregano
flat-leaved parsley
freshly ground pepper

Stone the olives, cut the butter into small pieces and combine in a food
processor. Blend until the olive flesh and butter forms a smooth paste. Add the
thyme, oregano and pepper.
    Transfer to a small bowl or 4 ramekins of contrasting colour, and garnish
with flat-leaved parsley before serving. The rillettes will keep well for a few
days if refrigerated.

Serves 8

Sauces and Savouries

BASIL AND RAW TOMATO SAUCE

Serve with Cold Aubergine Soufflé, p60, and Green Tomato
and Black Plum Salad, p57, or Yellow and Green
Courgette Salad, p66.

1½ lb (675 g) large tomatoes
1 purple garlic clove
3 sprigs fresh basil
4 sprigs flat-leaved parsley, chopped
a little dry marjoram or oregano
4 tablespoons fruity olive oil
salt and freshly ground pepper

To peel the tomatoes, immerse them for 1 minute in a bowl of boiling water.
Sieve the tomatoes and add the pressed garlic clove. (If the clove is not fresh,
cut it lengthways and remove the green shoot.) Add half the basil leaves (torn
in pieces), parsley, marjoram or oregano and olive oil. Stir, season and chill
until needed. Garnish with the remaining basil, and serve.

Makes 1 pt (550 ml)

◆

MUSTARD AND TARRAGON SAUCE

Serve this sauce with French Bean and Mushroom Salad,
p57, cold fish, steamed potatoes or a prawn and radish salad.

2 egg yolks
1 tablespoon French mustard
3 tablespoons olive oil
4 fl oz (120 ml) sour cream
3-4 tarragon sprigs
salt and white pepper

In a bowl, start beating the egg yolks and French mustard. Add the olive oil in a
thin stream, until emulsified and thickened. Add the sour cream and the finely
chopped tarragon, reserving a few whole leaves for the garnish. Season with
salt and white pepper. Garnish with tarragon leaves and cover until needed.

Makes 8 fl oz (250 ml)

Desserts and Cakes

CONFITURE DE VIEUX GARÇON

The name of this old-fashioned recipe is French for 'old
bachelor's jam', perhaps implying that it will perk up
sagging spirits. A large, tall, glass jar in which to mature
the fruit and spirit is ideal, or use a glazed earthenware
crock or enamelled container.

Gradually fill the container with layers of fruit in season, starting at the
beginning of the summer, and topping up with fruit spirit (Eau de Vie), rum or
brandy after each addition. Peaches, apricots and plums should be stoned, and
halved or quartered. (Leave cherries whole, with their stalks on, before
immersion in spirit.) Each layer may be lightly sprinkled with sugar. At the
end of the summer the fruit should be left for a few months to macerate and
become impregnated with alcohol; by then it will have become discoloured. It
will be ready to eat at the beginning of winter.

Serve in small glasses, with a spoon, as a topping with ice cream or
sandwiched, with whipped cream, between shortbread biscuits.

◆

STRAWBERRY AND KIWI SALAD

Prepare this salad at the last minute as the fruit must be
fresh and visually appealing. A little raspberry or pear
liqueur adds a sophisticated touch, and pepper brings out
the strawberries' flavour.

1 lb (450 g) strawberries, hulled
2 kiwi fruit, peeled
juice of ½ lemon
a little fruit liqueur
2-3 sprigs fresh mint
freshly ground black pepper

Place the strawberries in a glass bowl, preferably, the bottom filled with
crushed ice. Cut the kiwi fruit into thick slices; place them decoratively in the
bowl. Pour over the lemon juice and liqueur, tuck in the sprigs of mint.
Sprinkle with pepper and serve.

Serves 4

Confiture de Vieux Garçon, partially prepared Strawberry
and Kiwi Salad, Exotic Fruit and Berry Salad

EXOTIC FRUIT AND BERRY SALAD

Here, the flavour is enhanced by lime juice and
Angostura bitters.

6 passion-fruit
1 mango, peeled and sliced
8 oz (225 g) blueberries
8 oz (225 g) raspberries
8 oz (225 g) blackberries
1 tablespoon castor sugar
juice and grated zest of 1 lime
1 teaspoon Angostura bitters
6-8 basil leaves

Cut the passion-fruit in half, and scoop out the flesh into a sieve placed over a
bowl. Sieve the flesh, discarding the seeds. Combine the passion-fruit flesh
with the mango and berries, sprinkle with sugar, then add the lime juice and
zest and the bitters. Toss gently and chill for at least 2 hours.

Just before serving, tuck in the whole basil leaves as decoration.

Serves 6

◆

GOOSEBERRY CURD

Store this curd in a refrigerator, and eat it within a month.
Serve on toast at tea-time or as a filling for a shortcrust pie.

1 lb (450 g) gooseberries
4 oz (120 g) butter
8 oz (225 g) castor sugar
2 eggs, lightly beaten

Top, tail and wash the gooseberries, and place them, still wet, into a heavy
enamelled saucepan. Stew the fruit until soft, then press through a sieve. Stir
in the butter and sugar, and add the eggs. Gently heat the purée mixture,
stirring constantly, until it is thickened and coats the back of a spoon. Cool a
little and pour into a warmed jar, cover and label.

Makes about 1 lb (450 g)

Desserts and Cakes

TOMATO CHEESE

'Cheese' is the old-fashioned word for a preserve
made from fruit. The fruit is stewed and then strained –
the juice is kept to make jelly, and the remaining purée of
pulp becomes the 'cheese'. The process used here is a little
different but the end result resembles the traditional
'cheese'. It is particularly good eaten with Quick Fromage
Blanc, p68, or with Wensleydale cheese, and goes well,
too, with cold meat or poultry. Adding a few coriander
seeds – about a teaspoon, powdered in a mortar – will give
a spicy note.

2 lb (1 kg) tomatoes
1 lb (450 g) apples
1 lb (450 g) preserving sugar for each
pint (550 ml) tomato and apple pulp
juice and rind of one lemon
oil for greasing

Quarter the tomatoes and apples and simmer until soft and pulpy, rather than
wet, then press through a nylon – not metal – sieve. Measure the pulp and place
it, with the juice and grated rind of lemon, in a preserving pan. Add the sugar
using the proportions given above.

Simmer gently, stirring frequently, until the sugar is dissolved. Increase the
heat slightly and, stirring occasionally to keep the pulp from sticking to the
bottom of the pan, simmer the purée for about 1½ hours. Beware of hot
spatterings from the pan.

Test a little of the pulp on a small plate; once it sets, it is ready. Pour into
warmed jam jars or a small mould.

Makes 2 jars

SHIMMERING RED AND GREEN GOOSEBERRIES

The gooseberries are entrapped in a lightly set
jelly which is flavoured with ginger wine and lime.
The glossy dish is dotted with red and green gooseberries
and blackcurrants.

4 oz (120 g) sugar
1-2 elderflower heads (optional)
1 lb (450 g) green gooseberries, very ripe
juice of ¹/₂ lime
8 oz (225 g) red gooseberries, very ripe
5-6 redcurrant and/or blackcurrant sprigs
1 packet (¹/₂ tablespoon) gelatine
5 fl oz (150 ml) ginger wine
lightly sweetened creamed smetana (optional)

Make a syrup with 1 pt (550 ml) water and sugar. Add the elderflower heads, if using, and leave to infuse for 20 minutes.

Meanwhile, top and tail the green gooseberries and reserve. Strain the flavoured syrup, then pour it back into the pan, adding the lime juice and green gooseberries. Simmer for about 20 minutes or until the gooseberries are softened but still hold their shape.

With a slotted spoon, carefully place the cooked gooseberries in a porcelain pie dish. Place the red gooseberries here and there, and the redcurrants and/or blackcurrants, stripped from their stalks, for a pretty, speckled effect.

Sprinkle the gelatine over the hot syrup and let it dissolve. Strain, then cool the syrup for a few minutes; stir in the ginger wine. When the syrup starts to set pour it slowly over the fruit and chill until needed. Serve, if you wish, with a jug of creamed smatana lightly sweetened.

Serves 6

Shimmering Red and Green Gooseberries,
Gooseberry Curd, Tomato Cheese

PHYSALIS CHEESECAKE

This is an uncooked cheesecake flavoured with saffron and decorated with Physalis fruits (Cape gooseberries) and frosted mint leaves. Serve with Eau de Rhubarb, p79, or Grapefruit and Mint Drink, p79.

1 lb (450 g) cream cheese
8 oz (225 g) curd cheese
1 tablespoon sour cream or yoghurt
1 teaspoon vanilla extract
2 saffron stigmas, powdered in a mortar
2 egg whites
a pinch of salt
7 large mint leaves
6 tablespoons castor sugar
oil for greasing
7 physalis fruits (Cape gooseberries)

Bring the cream cheese, curd cheese and sour cream (or yoghurt) to room temperature, then beat until smooth. Add the vanilla and saffron. Reserve. Beat the egg whites and salt to a soft peak. Brush the mint leaves with egg white and dredge with sugar. Place the leaves on greaseproof paper and dry in a cool oven for 30 minutes or until crystallized.

Meanwhile, in a heavy saucepan, make a syrup with the remaining sugar and 2 tablespoons of water. Boil for 3 minutes, then pour it, in a thin stream, over the egg whites, beating at high speed. The mixture will swell into a glossy mass. Beat for a further 5 minutes after the syrup has been incorporated. Fold the 'cooked' meringue into the cheese mixture and pour into an oiled pie ring placed on a round serving dish. Refrigerate for a few hours, or up to 48 hours.

Just before serving, run a sharp blade around the metal ring, then remove it. Decorate the cake with the frosted mint leaves and the physalis fruit, turning out their delicate, husk-like calyces.

Serves 6–8

Physalis Cheesecake, Nectarine Pie, Eau de Rhubarbe,
Grapefruit and Mint Drink

Desserts and Cakes

NECTARINE PIE

Here filo dough pastry leaves are used to make a fragile
frill around the luscious centre. Eau de Rhubarbe, p79,
makes a nice accompaniment.

10 sheets filo dough
6 oz (180 g) coarsely ground almonds
2 oz (60 g) chopped pistachio nuts
3 tablespoons dry breadcrumbs
8 oz (225 g) apricot jam
1 tablespoon Grand Marnier or Triple Sec
about 3 oz (85 g) unsalted butter, melted and cooled
1 heaped tablespoon icing sugar
4-5 ripe nectarines

Preheat the oven to 375°F/190°C/Gas 5

Trim the filo dough sheets into a square shape, stack them between 2 pieces of waxed paper, and cover with a damp cloth.

In a small bowl combine the ground almonds, chopped pistachio nuts and dry breadcrumbs. In a small saucepan melt three quarters of the apricot jam with the orange liqueur and 1 tablespoon of melted butter over a gentle heat, stirring until well blended. Reserve.

Brush a deep 8 in (20 cm) plain pie tin with some of the remaining butter. Fit one filo leaf into the tin, pressing it flat against the sides and bottom with a brush dipped in butter, letting the edges overlap. Layer 3 more sheets, brushing each one lightly with butter. (Each leaf should be placed at a different angle from the previous one, proceeding in a clockwise fashion.) Sprinkle one-third of the nut mixture over the bottom, dribble over one-third of the apricot mixture, and add 2 more filo sheets, brushing each one with butter. Repeat the operation twice more, finishing with a leaf on top, which is brushed with butter. You should now have a kind of nest in which the nectarine wedges will be placed. To hold up the petal-like overlapping filo dough, wrap the mould with a large piece of foil.

Bake the pie crust in the preheated oven for 30-35 minutes or until the filo leaves are a golden colour. (If the filo sheets brown too quickly, cover them loosely with foil.) Let the pie crust cool on a rack for 10 minutes. Invert it gently onto a large tin, then invert again onto a serving dish. Sift the icing sugar around the pie's frill. Cut each nectarine into 8 wedges, and place in the pastry crust. Preheat and strain the remaining apricot mixture and brush the apricots with it. Serve the pie lukewarm.

Serves 6-8

Drinks

GRAPEFRUIT AND MINT DRINK

This non-alcoholic cocktail is very refreshing and healthy.
If you can't get pink grapefruit, colour the drink with
grenadine syrup, to tinge it with pink. Do not extract the
juice in advance as it would quickly lose its lovely clean taste.
If you like, serve this drink with the Nectarine Pie, p78,
or Physalis Cheesecake, p76, to end a meal.

4 large pink grapefruit
1 tablespoon castor sugar or
1 tablespoon of grenadine syrup
crushed ice
6 mint sprigs

Cut in 2 and extract the juice from the grapefruit, stir in the castor sugar (or
grenadine syrup). Strip off the leaves of 2 mint sprigs and cut them finely with
scissors. Add to the grapefruit juice.

Take 4 tall glasses, half-fill them with crushed ice, pour over the minted
drink, and stick a mint sprig into each glass. Drink without delay.

Serves 4

◆

EAU DE RHUBARBE

This is a pleasant drink to serve outdoors at tea-time. It
would be nice with Physalis Cheesecake, p76, or
Nectarine Pie, p78.

1 lb (450 g) rhubarb
5 oz (150 g) castor sugar
borage flowers (optional)

Bring 4 pints (2 litres) water to the boil. Cut the rhubarb stalks in ½ in (1 cm)
pieces and place them with the sugar in an earthenware jug or bowl. Pour over
the boiling water. Leave to macerate for 48 hours. Strain the mixture into a
large jug and chill.

Serve in large tumblers with ice cubes and, if you can get them, a few borage
flowers on top.

Serves 6

AUTUMN

Autumn is a transitional time for entertaining, with children returning to school, friends returning from holidays, and temporarily broken threads of friendship being taken up again. In early autumn, the feeling is still very much that of summer, with the afternoons and early evenings warm enough to enjoy a meal outdoors.

The produce from your own garden, and from the shops, starts autumn in a summery way, too, with peaches and plums at their ripest and most fragrant. Autumn-fruiting raspberries and strawberries extend summer's delights, and, until the first frost, you might have freshly picked sweetcorn, green peppers and their pretty red and yellow counterparts. Menus will be extravagant in their use of fresh ingredients – freshly picked herbs, fruit and vegetables – simply because it is a race against the seasonal clock.

Sooner or later, the feeling will change; cooler weather begins, and the focus of life, for family and friends alike, shifts indoors, with the warmth and glow of the fireside overtaking the pleasures of eating in the garden. Ingredients change, and the scale of presentation, too, as cold weather brings on appetites. Pumpkins, marrows and root vegetables begin to make an appearance, first in a supporting role to summer salad vegetables, and, eventually, as 'stars' in their own right. Autumn also means the advent of wild mushrooms, nuts and game, a trio that makes the passing of summer somehow less sad.

In the kitchen, autumn is a time for stocktaking, and for preserving the best of autumn's bounty. Wild mushrooms, herbs, quinces and fruit of all sort, need to be dried or preserved in oil and vinegar, made into pickles, jams, chutneys or relishes, to extend the pleasures of autumn into winter. And though nothing equals using produce freshly gathered, preserving fresh produce with your own selection of flavourings and spices, with recipes that are yours alone, and presenting them as part of uniquely devised menus, are an inherent part of creative cookery, and a pleasurable one.

COTTAGE CHEESE TERRINE

Serve this terrine with toasted bread or rye biscuits, or with Turnip, Red Potato and Watercress Salad, p101.

8 oz (225 g) cottage cheese
4 oz (120 g) Emmenthal or Wensleydale cheese
3 hard-boiled eggs
2 tongue slices
15 juniper berries
salt and freshly ground pepper
a few chives, finely chopped

Put the cottage cheese in a bowl. Coarsely grate the Emmenthal or Wensleydale and add it to the bowl. Chop finely – but do not mash – the hard-boiled eggs. Cut the tongue into small squares. Crush 3 juniper berries in a mortar. Add all these ingredients to the cheese mixture and stir until well blended. Season to taste. Pour into a pretty terrine dish and refrigerate for an hour or so, to allow the mixture to become firm and the berries to impart their fragrance to the terrine. Sprinkle with the finely chopped chives and remaining juniper berries.

Serves 4

CORN AND CHEESE SOUFFLÉ

The use of breadcrumbs instead of flour gives the soufflé a
great lightness. The Double Gloucester cheese has a
mature flavour and bright colour which goes well with the
corn. When the soufflé is cut through it shows green
speckles and pink dots. Try it with Beetroot Salad, p100,
and Steamed Monkfish with Fennel, p91.

4 eggs, separated
1/2 teaspoon Worcestershire sauce
10 fl oz (280 ml) hot milk
2 oz (60 g) butter, softened, plus extra for greasing
4 oz (120 g) white breadcrumbs
8 oz (225 g) Double Gloucester cheese, cut into small cubes
1 tablespoon pink peppercorns, lightly crushed (optional)
2 tablespoons flat-leaved parsley, roughly chopped
11.5 oz (325 g) tin corn nibblets, drained
salt and freshly ground pepper

Preheat the oven to 350°F/180°C/Gas 4
Beat the egg yolks, Worcestershire sauce and hot milk. Season. Add the
softened butter, breadcrumbs, cubed cheese, pink peppercorns, if using, and
chopped parsley. In a blender, blend the mixture until smooth.

Whisk the egg whites until very stiff, then gently fold into the cheese
mixture and add a third of the corn nibblets. Pour half into a lightly buttered, 2
pint (1 litre) soufflé dish. Spread with the remaining corn nibblets and pour
over the rest of the soufflé mixture. Bake in the oven for 30 to 35 minutes or
until the soufflé is golden brown on top. Serve immediately.

Serves 6

Eggs, Cheeses and Grains

BAKED APPLE AND GOAT CHEESE

This is a very simple recipe which relies on the prime
quality of all the ingredients. The centre of the goat cheese
melts, but the crust holds its shape. It is delicious with
Yellow and Red Marinated Peppers, p103, and Sautéed
Potatoes with Egg Yolks, p86.

3 cooking apples
oil for greasing
3 small round goat cheese,
about 1½ in (4 cm) diameter
2 tablespoons double cream
1-2 thyme sprigs
cayenne pepper

Preheat the oven to 400°F/200°C/Gas 6
Peel and core the apples, keeping them whole (a metal corer will do the task in a
few seconds). Cut the apples in 3 horizontally. Place the slices in a greased
ovenproof.dish. Cut the small cheeses in 3 and place on top of the apples.
Dribble over the cream. Tuck the sprigs of thyme between the cheese-topped
apples. Bake for about 6 to 8 minutes. Add a dash of cayenne pepper and serve
immediately.

Makes 9 slices

Baked Apple and Goat Cheese,
Sautéed Potatoes with Egg Yolks, Yellow
and Red Marinated Peppers

SAUTÉED POTATOES WITH EGG YOLKS

Here half-shells are used as cups for the yolks.
I like to use an old egg-rack to bring the half-shells to the
table, each guest taking a yolk-filled shell. The potatoes,
tossed in the yolk, become coated with a golden glaze.
Yellow and Red Marinated Peppers, p103, would
complement nicely the rich taste of the sautéed potatoes
and yolks.

4 eggs, preferably free range
1¹/₂ lb (675 g) waxy potatoes
about 1 oz (30 g) butter
about 3 tablespoons olive oil
2 garlic cloves, cut in 2
salt and freshly ground pepper
a few chives, finely chopped

Separate the eggs, carefully breaking the shells in half. Select the 4 nicest halves
as they will be brought to the table. Save the whites for another use, such as a
soufflé, and replace each yolk inside the reserved half shells. Place on an egg
rack or in individual egg cups; antique, non-matching ones would look
attractive. Reserve.

Peel the potatoes and cut into cubes. Heat the butter and oil in a frying pan
and when very hot, put in the potatoes and garlic cloves cut in 2. Season. Sauté
the potatoes until golden on all sides, but still soft in the centre, tossing from
time to time. This takes about 15 to 20 minutes, and all the fat should be
absorbed. Drain the potatoes on kitchen paper and transfer to a serving dish.
Garnish with the chopped chives and serve at once with the egg-yolk 'cups'.

Serves 4

Eggs, Cheeses and Grains

STILTON AND PECAN MOUSSE

It is a good idea to use the end of a whole smallish Stilton cheese; the crust becomes the container for the mousse. Serve with Poulet en Papillotte, p94.

3 oz (85 g) Stilton cheese
3 oz (85 g) unsalted butter
2 oz (60 g) pecan nuts, lightly toasted
1 egg
4 fl oz (120 ml) sour cream or creamed smatana
salt
cream of tartar
cayenne pepper
a few bay leaves

Cut the Stilton and butter in small pieces and beat until thoroughly blended. Coarsely chop the nuts, reserving a few halves for garnish. Separate the egg white and yolk, placing each one in a mixing bowl. To the egg yolk add the cheese mixture and the sour cream or creamed smatana. Whip the egg white with a pinch each of salt and cream of tartar, until it stands in soft peaks. With a spatula, fold in a quarter of the egg white to the cheese mixture, then the rest, incorporating the chopped pecan nuts at the same time. Transfer to the Stilton shell or, failing that, a terrine dish. Garnish with a breath of cayenne pepper, the reserved pecan halves and the bay leaves tucked here and there.

Serves 4-6

MUSTARD BREAD

This wholemeal bread is made with coarse-grain
mustard. The addition of cracked wheat, or 'burghul' –
parboiled cracked wheat which is often used in Middle
Eastern cooking – gives an extra chewy texture to the
bread. You can buy a dried yeast which is blended directly
with the flour, thus eliminating the initial stage of
fermentation in water. If you can't get burghul, substitute
leftover rice. Serve it with Crème d'Endive et Laitue,
p102, or Cheddar cheese and Pickled Quinces, p120.
Bread keeps for months if sliced and frozen; take the slices
as and when you need them.

4 tablespoons cracked wheat or burghul
1 tablespoon olive oil, plus extra for greasing
12 oz (340 g) wholemeal flour, plus extra for sprinkling
4 oz (120 g) strong white flour
1 packet dried yeast
3 tablespoons coarse-grain mustard
1 tablespoon maple syrup or malt extract
2 scant teaspoons sea salt

Soak the cracked wheat (or burghul) in 4 to 5 tablespoons of tepid water. While
you prepare the bread, it will swell up and absorb the water. When all the water
is absorbed, stir in the olive oil.

Mix the 2 flours and dried yeast in a bowl. Dissolve the mustard, maple
syrup or malt extract and sea salt in 10 fl oz (280 ml) warm water. Gradually
pour the liquid mixture over the dry ingredients, incorporating it roughly with
a wooden spoon. When the dough gets too stiff and sticky to work, turn it onto a
board sprinkled with more wholemeal flour and knead for 10 minutes or until
the dough is smooth and pliable. Halfway through the kneading, incorporate
the cracked wheat. Shape the dough into a ball, pat it all over with oil and place
in a 1 lb (450g), greased bread tin, filling it about three-quarters full. Cover, set
in a warm place and leave to rise until doubled in bulk (2 to 3 hours if left at
room temperature).

Preheat the oven to 350°F/180°C/Gas 4 and bake the bread for 45 minutes.
The loaf should sound hollow when removed from the tin and tapped on the
bottom. Leave to cool on a rack.

Makes 1 loaf

Eggs, Cheeses and Grains

QUAIL EGGS WITH WILD MUSHROOMS

For this recipe, it would be nice to use a combination of
two different types of mushroom like, for example,
grey-beige oyster mushrooms (*Pleurotus ostreatus*) and
yellow chanterelles (*Cantharellus cibarius*), or white
button mushrooms with the black horn-of-plenty
(*Craterellus cornucopioides*).
The dish looks pretty as the tiny eggs and wild mushrooms
are placed in the centre of some alfalfa sprouts arranged in a
nest-like fashion. Serve with game, such as Pheasant
with Citronella and Wild Rice, p98.

18 quail eggs
2 oz (60 g) butter
8 oz (225 g) of each mushroom species
1-2 garlic shavings
3 packets alfalfa sprouts
salt and freshly ground pepper

Place the eggs in a pan and cover with cold water. Bring to a boil and cook for
exactly 2 minutes. Run under cold water and peel 10 eggs.

Melt the butter in a pan, add the mushrooms (wiped clean, and sliced if
large) and 1 or 2 garlic shavings. Season. Sauté for 5 to 7 minutes.

Meanwhile, arrange the alfalfa sprouts in a nest and place the peeled eggs in
the centre; I do this in a shallow glazed bowl or wicker tray, or on an old bread
board. When the mushrooms are ready, pile them amongst the peeled eggs
and garnish with the unpeeled ones.

Serves 6

Fish and Shellfish

STEAMED MONKFISH WITH FENNEL

Here the fish is steamed, then wrapped in a Swiss chard
leaf. You can substitute spinach leaves for the Swiss
chard. Serve with Fluffy Anis Sauce, p107.

1½ lb (675 g) boned monkfish
1 tablespoon melted butter
1 teaspoon fennel seeds
8 large Swiss chard or spinach leaves
salt and freshly ground pepper

Cut the monkfish in 4 slices. Brush each piece with butter, season, and sprinkle
with fennel seeds. Steam for 6 to 8 minutes. Remove and cool slightly.
Wrap each piece in 2 washed leaves, and return, seam down, to the steamer.
Steam for a further 2 minutes. Serve, accompanied by the sauce.

Serves 4

STEAMED OKRA WITH PRAWN BUTTER

Okra are also called lady's fingers or gumbo.

1 lb (450 g) small okra
½ pint (250 ml) prawns
2 oz (60 g) butter
1 teaspoon lemon juice
4 small spring onions, cut in julienne strips
salt and freshly ground pepper

Pare off the okra's stalks without cutting into the pods. Wash and pat dry. Shell
all the prawns but 3. Heat the debris in the butter until it starts to foam. Cool for
15 to 20 minutes, then sieve, gathering every last drop of butter. Transfer to a
clean saucepan, adding the lemon juice, salt and pepper.
Steam the okra for 8 minutes, or until just soft. Reheat the butter. Place the
okra on a serving dish with the peeled prawns. Pour over the butter and garnish
with spring onion strips and unshelled prawns.

Serves 4-6

Steamed Monkfish with Fennel, Fluffy Anis Sauce,
Corn and Cheese Soufflé, Beetroot Salad

POLENTA AND BACALHAU

'Polenta' is the name of a traditional Italian porridge made from maize meal and originating from the region of Piemont. 'Bacalhau' is the Portuguese word for salt cod. Serve this rather earthy dish with a simple salad and a good Sancerre wine.

1¹/₂ lb (675 g) salt cod
1¹/₂ pints (840 ml) chicken stock
1 teaspoon dried oregano or marjoram
8 oz (225 g) polenta, medium size
2 tablespoons butter
5 fl oz (150 ml) double cream
a few nutmeg gratings
freshly ground pepper
2 tablespoons chopped flat-leaved parsley
2-3 coppa slices or 3 oz (100 g) small black olives

Soak the salt cod in cold water for 24 hours, changing the water several times. After the last rinse, pat dry and cut the fish in smallish pieces, discarding any bones. Bring the stock and oregano or marjoram to a boil, and pour in the polenta, in a stream. Add 1 tablespoon of butter, and stir constantly to avoid lumps. In 4 to 5 minutes the polenta should be firm but not stiff. Transfer to a greased cake tin and leave to cool.

Heat 1 tablespoon of butter in a pan and when it starts to bubble, add the salt cod. Stir constantly, until the fish disintegrates into a creamy mass. Add the double cream, nutmeg and pepper. Blend well and remove from the heat.

To serve, cut the polenta into thickish slices then place them, overlapping slightly, in an oblong serving dish. Spread the bacalhau mixture over the polenta, then scatter the coppa, cut into long strands, and parsley on top, or tuck, here and there, a few black olives. This dish can be reheated in the oven, covered with foil.

Serves 10

Polenta and Bacalhau, Cottage Cheese Terrine,
Turnip, Red Potato and Watercress Salad

Meat, Poultry and Game

POULET EN PAPILLOTTE

The chicken is first marinated, then cooked in a
greaseproof paper case. This is a very light dish which
goes well with Stilton and Pecan Mousse, p87. The tightly
closed paper parcels are presented to each guest to open,
which releases the pungent aroma. The chicken may be
replaced with rabbit.

6 chicken thighs
½ tablespoon sesame oil
1 tablespoon sunflower oil, plus extra for greasing
1 teaspoon soya sauce
salt and freshly ground pepper
1 lemon
6 large sage leaves or 6 small sage sprigs

You will need 6 greaseproof paper circles about 12 in (30 cm) in diameter,
greased lightly on one side.

Remove the skin from the chicken thighs and make 2 slits in each thigh with
a sharp knife. Place in a bowl. For the marinade, blend the sesame and
sunflower oil, soya sauce and pepper, and rub all over the chicken pieces.
Leave in the refrigerator for up to 12 hours, tossing them once or twice,

Preheat the oven to 375°F/190°C/Gas 5. Drain the chicken. Cut the lemon
into 6 slices, discarding the 2 ends. Place each chicken thigh on one half of the
greased side of a greaseproof paper circle. Season with pepper and salt and
place a lemon slice on top, then a sage leaf, or sprig. Fold over and crimp the
edges to seal the half-circle-shaped papillotte.

Bake in the oven for 15 to 20 minutes. Serve the puffed-up papillottes
immediately. Break them open at the table, letting the aromatic steam escape.

If you like, boil the marinade with a little more oil for a few minutes, and
dribble over toasted bread slices. Serve them separately in a basket with the
chicken, or cut into pieces and use as croûtons on a green salad. If you fail to get
greaseproof paper, replace it with foil, but the final effect will not be so
attractive.

Serves 6

Poulet en Papillote, Steamed Okra with
Prawn Butter, Stilton and Pecan Mousse

*Smoked Quails with Pink Yams, Mustard
Bread, Crème d'Endive et Laitue*

SMOKED QUAILS WITH PINK YAMS

In this recipe, the quails are cooked in a pink
yam gratin and their flavour and juice impregnate the
yams. Despite the long cooking time, the quails will keep
moist, as they are steamed in the gratin. Buy Spanish
yams (Malaga Pink) which have a terracotta-colored skin
and bright flesh. You will need a deep earthenware dish,
so the quails can be completely covered with the yams.
Crème d'Endive et Laitue, p102, complements the rich
taste of this dish.

6 smoked quails
about 6 pink yams, medium size
1 garlic clove
1 oz (30 g) butter
salt and freshly ground pepper
1 whole nutmeg
a little cinnamon
10 fl oz (280 ml) rich milk
12 oz (340 g) double cream

Preheat the oven to 350°F/180°C/Gas 4
Peel, wash and pat dry the yams, and cut in thin slices (a task quickly done with
a food processor). Rub an ovenproof earthenware dish with the peeled garlic
clove and butter the dish lavishly. Put the quails inside, evenly spaced, make a
yam layer, season it with a few nutmeg gratings, a pinch of cinnamon, salt and
pepper. Repeat the operation, making successive seasoned yam layers. Mix
together the milk and cream and pour over the dish. Dot the top with the
remaining butter and bake for about 2 hours. Serve immediately.

Serves 6

Meat, Poultry and Game

PHEASANT WITH CITRONELLA AND WILD RICE

Citronella, sometimes called lemon grass, is often used in
South-East Asian cooking. You can substitute lemon
balm, lemon verbena or lemon rind for the lemon grass.
Serve with Sauce with Three Berries, p106.

1 large pheasant	**For the stuffing**
8 bacon rashers	*4 petit Suisse cheese*
about 12 vine leaves	*1 lemon grass or 2 tablespoons*
2 small parsnips	*dried lemon grass*
6 small carrots	*1 garlic clove*
8oz (225 g) wild rice	*4 mushrooms*
2 oz (60 g) butter	*fresh thyme*
fresh thyme	*salt and freshly ground pepper*

Preheat the oven to 475°F/240°C/Gas 9

In a bowl prepare the stuffing. Mash the cream cheese and add the citronella
(the outer blades removed and shredded) reserving a little for the rice. Shave
off a little of the garlic clove. Wipe clean and roughly chop the mushrooms and
add the thyme, salt and pepper. Thoroughly mix the ingredients. Reserve. Fill
the 2 halves of a chicken brick with cold water and soak for 10 minutes.

Clean and wipe dry the inside of the pheasant, then stuff the cavity and sew
closed or secure with a skewer. Season and cover the breast, lattice-like, with the
bacon. Wrap the pheasant with vine leaves and tie securely with string.

Empty the water from the brick halves, lining 1 of them with foil. Peel and
clean the parsnips and carrots and cut them, lengthways, into large sticks.
Place the vegetables at the bottom of the lined brick half and put the pheasant
on top. Cover and bake for 1½ hours.

Meanwhile place the rice in a pan and cover with 20 fl oz (450 ml) water.
Bring to a boil, reduce the heat and simmer for 30 to 35 minutes. Drain and add
the butter, thyme, salt, pepper and remaining citronella. Toss and keep warm.

When the pheasant is ready, transfer it to a large serving dish. Surround
with the drained parsnips and carrots, and wild rice. Serve the remaining juice
in a jug. The pheasant is freed from the vine leaves and carved at the table.
Scoop out a little of the stuffing with each helping.

Serves 3-4

*Partially prepared Pheasant with Citronella and Wild Rice, Sauce with
Three Berries, Quail Eggs with Wild Mushrooms*

BEETROOT SALAD

The beetroots in this salad are sliced with a large serrated
knife in a sawing motion, thus leaving an attractive
chevron pattern. The slices are brushed with oil, so
emphasizing the design. The sharpness of the sorrel goes
well with the beetroots' sweetness, and both flavours go
well with Corn and Cheese soufflé, p83. I think that, from
the point of view of flavour, beetroots should be baked
rather than boiled.

1 lb (450 g) uncooked beetroots of even size
1 tablespoon walnut oil
salt
a few sorrel leaves

Preheat the oven to 350°F/180°/Gas 4
Trim off the beetroot stems, leaving on about 1 in (2.5 cm) Wrap the beetroot
loosely in foil and bake them for an hour. Let cool a little, then, with rubber
gloves on, cut off the whiskers and stalks, and slip off the skins. Cut with a
serrated knife and arrange the slices, slightly overlapping, on a shallow dish.
Brush with the oil and sprinkle with very little salt. Just before serving, shred
the sorrel leaves and use them for garnishing.

Serves 4

TURNIP, RED POTATO AND WATERCRESS SALAD

This salad looks quite dramatic, the green watercress contrasting prettily with the pink-tinged, white turnips and the red potatoes. Try to get baby turnips which are usually sold in a bunch with their leaves on. I find that it is better not to use any dressing on the watercress, otherwise it loses its sharp, peppery taste.

1 lb (450 g) small turnips of even size
8 oz (225 g) small red-skinned potatoes
2-3 watercress bunches
1 teaspoon French mustard
2 teaspoons wine vinegar
salt and freshly ground pepper
3 tablespoons olive oil

If you get baby turnips they will not need peeling, just remove the stalks and leaves. Clean and pat dry. Steam the whole turnips in a Chinese bamboo steamer for 6 to 8 minutes, depending on their size. Immediately cool under cold running water for a few minutes, then cut into quarters.

Steam the unpeeled potatoes for 15 minutes. Cut in 2 and reserve. Trim the ends of the watercress stems and discard any yellowed leaves.

Make the dressing as follows: using a fork, beat the mustard and vinegar, and season with salt and pepper. Still beating, gradually add the olive oil to emulsify the dressing, as for a mayonnaise. In a bowl, toss the turnips and potatoes in the dressing.

For serving, use a pretty dish. Start with the watercress, placed round the edge in a crown fashion, overlapping the rim. Then place in the centre a mixture of the potatoes and the turnips. If you like, use the turnip leaves for garnish too, tied in a little bunch and placed in the centre of the dish: otherwise use them to flavour a soup.

Serves 6

Vegetables and Salads

CRÈME d'ENDIVE ET LAITUE

This soup is very creamy and has the unusual combination
of cooked Belgian endive and lettuce. It looks pretty
served in a hollowed-out pumpkin in place of a tureen.
Use the scooped-out pumpkin flesh for making Vanishing
Pumpkin, p110.

1 lb (450 g) Belgian endives
2 lettuces
8 oz (225 g) floury potatoes, cooked and peeled
2 oz (60 g) butter
1 teaspoon castor sugar
2 pints (1 litre) chicken stock
nutmeg
5 fl oz (150 ml) double or sour cream
salt and freshly ground pepper

Trim, clean and pat dry the endives and lettuces. Chop into small pieces,
reserving 2 lettuce leaves for garnish. Cut the potatoes into small pieces. Melt
the butter in a large saucepan and sauté the chopped salads, sprinkled with the
sugar. Pour in the stock and add the cooked potatoes. Season with nutmeg, salt
and pepper. Cover and cook gently for about 20 minutes. Strain the soup
through a fine sieve or vegetable mill. Stir in the cream: double for a sweetish
taste, sour for a sharpish tang. Check the seasoning and adjust accordingly.
Pour the soup into a hollowed-out pumpkin or soup tureen and garnish with
the remaining lettuce leaves, cut in long shreds.

Serves 4-6

YELLOW AND RED MARINATED PEPPERS

This dish is very colourful and goes well with Baked
Apple and Goat Cheese, p84, cold meat and egg dishes,
but always serve it with plenty of wholemeal bread to mop
up the flavourful oil. If refrigerated, the peppers will keep
for over a week. For a variation, add or replace one of the
peppers with a green one.

2 large yellow peppers
2 large red peppers
4-5 tablespoons olive oil
3 garlic cloves
1 sprig fresh rosemary
salt and freshly ground pepper

Cook the peppers under a hot grill until they blacken and blister. Remove from
the grill and wrap in a dampened cloth or kitchen paper. Leave to cool, then
skin them, one by one, with a small, sharp knife. Cut off the stem and split the
pepper open, discarding all the seeds and white membranes. Rinse under cold
water to remove any bits of skin or seeds. Repeat the operation with the
remaining peppers.

Cut the peppers, lengthways, into long, slender strips, a little less than
½ in (1.5 cm) wide. Arrange in a shallow dish. Make a yellow and a red section,
slightly curving the pepper strips in order to follow the shape of the dish.
Dribble the oil all over until the peppers are thoroughly coated. Peel and shave
1 garlic clove evenly over the peppers. Split the others in 2, leaving their pretty,
iridescent skin on, and arrange on top. Season with salt and pepper. Place the
rosemary, cut in florets, over the peppers. Leave to marinate for at least 4
hours before serving.

Serves 4

Vegetables and Salads

PRESERVED MUSHROOMS

These mushrooms are delicious on their own with a good
wholemeal bread and the freshest butter, or added to a
salad. They go well, too, with cold meat or eggs. A jar
kept in the larder could transform a quick snack or a light
meal into a gourmet treat.

mushrooms
cider vinegar
salt
coriander seeds
black peppercorns
1 garlic clove
1 bay leaf
a sprig of thyme
a sprig of rosemary
olive oil

Simmer some mushrooms (several types would be a good idea) for 10 minutes
in a liquid made with half cider vinegar, half lightly salted water. Drain them
and leave to dry for six hours wrapped in a clean teacloth.

Inside a large jar, tightly pack some of the mushrooms together with a few
coriander seeds, 2 or 3 peppercorns, one whole garlic clove – unpeeled, but
lightly crushed, 1 bay leaf, a thyme sprig, a rosemary sprig and some fruity
olive oil. Continue adding the mushrooms, herbs and garlic until the jar is
three-quarters full. There should be plenty of olive oil flowing around the
mushrooms, herbs and spices. Get rid of any bubbles, to avoid mould
forming. Cover and keep in a cool place for a month. Do not keep for more than
three months (this is not too difficult!).

When the mushrooms are all eaten, the remaining seasoned, herbed oil
could be used in several ways: for cooking sautéed potatoes; in salad dressing;
and in mayonnaise.

Preserved Mushrooms, Cider Vinegar with
Honey, Pickled Quinces

Sauces and Savouries

SAUCE WITH THREE BERRIES

This fragrant sauce goes well with poultry or game such
as Pheasant with Citronella and Wild Rice, p98.

15 fl oz (420 ml) pheasant or other game stock
1 dessertspoon medlar or redcurrant jelly
2 teaspoons arrowroot
1 teaspoon juniper berries, lightly crushed
1 teaspoon green peppercorns, lightly crushed
1 teaspoon pink peppercorns, lightly crushed (optional)
salt and freshly ground pepper

In a small saucepan, heat the pheasant or game stock with the medlar or
redcurrant jelly until the latter has melted. In a small bowl, dissolve the
arrowroot in a little cold water and add it, stirring, to the stock. Add the berries
and peppercorns. Check the seasoning and adjust it to your taste. Reheat the
sauce until it boils and becomes clear. Transfer to a sauce-boat and serve.

Makes 15 fl oz (420 ml)

CIDER VINEGAR WITH HONEY

This is a flavoured, mild vinegar that is lovely in salad
dressings and in sweet-and-sour dishes. It is good, too, as
a refreshing drink – put a tablespoon of the flavoured
vinegar in a tall glass and top it with soda water and ice. If
put in pretty bottles, it also makes a nice present for
gourmet friends.

2 pt (1 litre) cider vinegar
4 oz (120 g) honey, preferably thyme flavoured
3 tablespoons fresh peppermint, finely chopped
1-2 large rosemary sprigs

In an enamelled pan, bring the vinegar to a gentle boil. Add the honey and the
mint, then lower the heat and simmer for 5 to 8 minutes. Strain through a
cheese muslin into clean, warmed, bottles with a rosemary sprig placed inside
and then cork. Leave to mature for 2 to 3 months before using.

Makes 2 pt (1 litre)

FLUFFY ANIS SAUCE

This easy-to-make, uncooked sauce is flavoured with
Pastis, an alcohol made from aniseed. The flavour, which
is not unlike fennel, goes well with Steamed Monkfish
with Fennel, p91. It is delicious, too, with vegetables.

2 eggs, separated
about 8 fl oz (225 ml) fruity olive oil
juice of ½ lemon
2 teaspoons Pastis
salt
white pepper
1 fennel sprig

Start the sauce as you would a mayonnaise, beating the egg yolks and pouring
in, first drop by drop, then in a thin stream, the olive oil. Keep beating until the
mixture is emulsified and rather too thick. Add the lemon juice and Pastis and
stir well. Season. Up to this stage, the sauce may be made a few hours in
advance: if so, cover it, but do not refrigerate.

Just before serving, whip the egg whites to a soft mass and fold into the
mayonnaise. Pour into a bowl, garnish with the fennel sprig, and serve.

Makes about 10 fl oz (250 ml)

◆

POMEGRANATE SAUCE

Serve this sharp-tasting sauce with Samali cake, p111.

3 pomegranates
juice of ½ lemon
4 oz (120 g) sugar

Peel off the skin and white membrane from one pomegranate, collecting the
whole seeds in a small bowl. Reserve.

Cut the other pomegranates in 2 and squeeze them, like an orange. Place
their juice, the lemon juice, 10 fl oz (280 ml) water and sugar into an enamelled
saucepan and boil for 2 minutes. Cool in the pan, then transfer, with the
reserved pomegranate seeds, to a pretty glass jug.

Makes 12 fl oz (360 ml)

BLUEBERRY HILL

This is delicious with Cold Spiced Tea, p121. If you are
lucky enough to have a source of wild bilberries, try
substituting these for the blueberries.

1 lb (450 g) Granny Smith apples
2 lb (1 kg) blueberries
juice and grated rind of 1 lime
4 oz (120 g) muscavado sugar
butter for greasing

For the topping
4 oz (120 g) wholemeal flour
4 oz (120 g) desiccated coconut
9 oz (265 g) sugar
1 teaspoon bicarbonate of soda
1 teaspoon ground cinnamon
a pinch of powdered mace
1½ oz (40 g) butter
1 egg, slightly beaten
sour cream, or Quick Fromage Blanc, p68, to serve

Preheat the oven to 375°F/190°C/Gas 5
Core and dice the apples, but do not peel them. In a large bowl, combine the
prepared apples, blueberries, lime juice and rind, and muscavado sugar.
Spread the mixture evenly in a greased 8 in (20 cm) casserole or glazed earthenware dish.

In another bowl, mix the wholemeal flour, desiccated coconut, 6 oz (170 g)
sugar, bicarbonate of soda, cinnamon and mace; cut in the butter with a pastry
blender until the mixture is crumbly. Stir in the beaten egg, and spread the
topping over the fruit, making a little hill in the centre.

Bake in the preheated oven for 25-30 minutes or until the top is a rich golden
colour. The fruit should still be a little firm, and their juice partly absorbed by
the crumbly topping.

Make a caramel with the remaining sugar and 1 tablespoon of water and
dribble it over the cooked crumble to make shiny patches.

Serves 8

Blueberry Hill, Cold Spiced Tea

Desserts and Cakes

VANISHING PUMPKIN

This pudding is so called because every time that it is
brought to the table, it disappears before I have a chance
to sample it. It has the texture of a custard and is a deep
cinnamon colour. The orange zest is an added fragrance
which enhances the flavours of the many spices used. Save
the shell for serving Crème d'Endive et Laitue, p102.

2 lb (1 kg) pumpkin flesh
juice and zest of 1/2 orange
1 in (2.5 cm) piece fresh ginger root
6 oz (170 g) sugar
1/2 teaspoon freshly grated nutmeg
1/2 teaspoon cinnamon
a pinch of clove
a pinch of pepper
2 eggs, lightly beaten
2 oz (60 g) crystallized angelica,
cut into thin sticks
sour cream, to serve

Preheat the oven to 375°F/190°C/Gas 5
Cut the pumpkin flesh into large chunks and place them in an enamelled pan
along with the orange juice and ginger piece cut in 2. Cook, covered, until the
pumpkin starts to release its juice, then uncover and cook, stirring often, until
reduced to a thick purée. Sieve into a bowl, and add the sugar, nutmeg,
cinnamon, clove, orange zest, pepper and, lastly the eggs, lightly beaten. Mix
until thoroughly blended, then pour the mixture into a generously buttered
10 in (25 cm) flan dish. Bake for 40 minutes, then switch off the heat and leave
the pudding for a further 30 minutes.
    When the pudding is ready, decorate with the angelica, making a wheel-like
pattern. Serve either at room temperature or chilled with a jug of sour cream.

Serves 8

SAMALI CAKE

Samali is a Greek cake made with semolina and saturated
with fragrant syrup. Serve with Pomegranate Sauce,
p107. The translucent pomegranate seeds have a sharp-
tasting juice which goes well with the samali. I sometimes
serve it, cut into bite-size pieces, with tea or coffee or as an
accompaniment to Pear and Marron Glacé Dôme, p113.
If you like, replace the syrup with Hymethus honey; it
comes from Mount Hymethus in Greece and has a
woody, resinous flavour. This cake will keep for days.

1 pint (550 ml) yoghurt
1 lb (450 g) medium semolina
8 oz (225 g) sugar
1 teaspoon bicarbonate of soda
butter for greasing
1 teaspoon baking powder
3 oz (90 g) whole almonds
For the syrup
1 lb (450 g) sugar
1 tablespoon rose- or
orange-flower water

Preheat the oven 350°F/180°C/Gas 4
In a large bowl, beat the yoghurt until smooth. Add the semolina, bicarbonate
of soda and baking powder and mix well. Pour the mixture into a lined and well
greased, 8 in (20 cm) square cake tin. Place the almonds on top, in a regular
pattern. Bake for 40 to 45 minutes.

When the cake is ready, remove it from the oven and let it cool. Meanwhile,
make a syrup by dissolving the sugar in 1 pt (550 ml) water, stirring until it is
dissolved completely, then boil for 2 to 3 minutes. Remove from the heat and
stir in the rose- or orange-flower water.

Cut the cake, still in the tin, into oblong, narrow slices and dribble over the
hot syrup until the cake is well impregnated. Cover with foil and keep in a
warm place for about an hour, so the flavours can mature, before serving.

Serves 12

PEAR AND MARRON GLACÉ DÔME

This pear ice cream is flavoured with pear liqueur and dotted with crystallized chestnuts (marrons glacés), then served on a tray made of coloured ice. Buy crystallized chestnuts at good delicatessens and Italian grocers.

18 crystallized chestnuts
2 lb (1 kg) Comice pears, ripe but firm
6 oz (170 g) castor sugar
1 teaspoon lemon juice
1 scant tablespoon pear liqueur
4 egg yolks
10 fl oz (280 ml) single cream

To make the ice base, three-quarters fill a cake tin 8 in (20 cm) in diameter with water. Add a few drops of food colouring and freeze for 4 hours or until completely set. Unmould, wrap in a plastic bag and replace in the freezer.

Crumble 9 crystallized chestnuts, leaving 9 whole, and reserve. Peel, quarter and core the pears, sprinkle with sugar, lemon juice and liqueur and let macerate while preparing the custard. In a large bowl, beat the egg yolks until frothy. Heat the cream and when nearly boiling, pour it onto the yolks, whisking. Place the bowl over a pan of gently boiling water and cook, stirring constantly, until the custard begins to thicken and coats the back of a spoon. Cool, stirring from time to time.

Purée the pears and their juice in a blender, then add the custard and blend until smooth. Transfer to a bowl with a diameter slightly smaller than the cake tin. Stir in the crumbled chestnuts and freeze.

An hour before serving, transfer the ice cream to the refrigerator to soften. Just before serving, put the coloured ice 'tray' on a folded napkin placed on a round dish (the napkin stops the ice slipping). Unmould the ice cream on top and decorate the top with the 5 whole crystallized chestnuts, and the sides with 8 chestnut halves.

Serves 10-12

Pear and Marron Glacé Dôme, Samali Cake served with
Pomegranate Sauce, Vanishing Pumpkin

SQUIRREL TREAT

The Kentish cob is a variety of filbert (*Corylus maxima*).
Nibble these treats with a glass or two of Sage Wine, p121.
Both are good to spark off animated conversations.

1 lb (450 g) Kentish cobs
1 tablespoon hazelnut oil
celery salt
freshly ground pepper

Break open and peel off most of the brown skin from the cobs; this is fun to do
with friends, while chatting. Place the shelled nuts in a small bowl. Toss with
the oil and season with celery salt and freshly ground pepper.

Serves 4-6

CAPOUN

This is a traditional, dried-fig cake from Provence.
'Capoun' is the dialect word for a round, wrapped-up parcel.

2 lb (1 kg) freshly dried figs
4 oz (120 g) whole almond or walnut halves
1 teaspoon fennel seeds
bay leaves
fresh fig leaves

Stuff some newly dried figs with a whole almond or walnut half each, then
place them in a cake tin, about 1½ in (4 cm) deep, criss-crossed with lengths of
rafia or string long enough to be wrapped and tied around the capoun, and
lined with fig leaves. Pile the figs in layers, placing fennel seeds and 1 or 2 bay
leaves amongst them. When the tin is filled, cover the top with more fig leaves,
folding down overlapping ones. Tie the raffia firmly. Put a plate of similar size
on top and press down with a heavy weight. Leave for a few days.

Invert the capoun on a board, decorate with fresh bay leaves tucked under
the raffia or string. Store for a few weeks, though it should keep for 3 months.

Serves 8

Capoun, Squirrel Treat, Sage Wine

Desserts, Cakes, and Drinks

TARTE TATIN À MA FAÇON

This is an upside-down tart which is made without pastry;
the apple slices are layered in a solid-based 8 in (20 cm)
cake tin, and baked for several hours. When the tart is
ready the fruit has reduced by half and the apples are
amber-coloured and a little translucent. Allspice, also
called Jamaican pepper, looks like a large peppercorn and
has a taste that resembles a mixture of several spices,
predominantly clove. The berry is very hard, so grind it in
a peppermill which is kept only for this purpose.

3 lb (1½ kg) Cox apples
about 1 oz (30 g) butter
about 1 tablespoon sugar
2 oz (60 g) large raisins
2 oz (60 g) currants
nutmeg
allspice
zest of ½ lemon
Greek yoghurt, to serve

Preheat the oven to 350°F/180°C/Gas 4

For this recipe I use a cake tin lined, bottom and sides, with greaseproof paper.
Peel and core the apples, then cut into thin slices. For the first layer, place the
slices in an even, flower-like pattern. For the second layer, arrange the apples
in concentric circles, the slices curve against the sides of the mould. Dot with a
little butter, scatter over some sugar, raisins and currants. Add a few nutmeg
shavings, 1 or 2 turns of the allspice mill and a little lemon zest. Repeat the
concentric apple layers using the other ingredients every 2 or 3 layers.

When the cake tin is filled right up to the rim, bake the tart for about 3 hours.
Half-way through, cover loosely with foil. After 3 hours switch off the oven and
leave the tart for another hour, to allow the apples to settle (the tart will have
reduced to half its original size). Invert the tart on a serving dish, peel off the
greaseproof paper and serve with a bowl of Greek yoghurt.

Serves 6-8

Desserts, Cakes, and Drinks

Gâteaux aux Noix Solognote

This cold dessert was served to me in Sologne, an area of
France situated across the Loire near Orléans. It is a
region of lakes and marshland, where walnut trees are
plentiful. You should use fresh walnuts in this recipe, if
you can. If fresh walnuts are not available, soak the
unshelled nuts overnight in warm milk; the milk penetrates
the shells and makes them easier to peel. The pudding is
decorated with bold chocolate curls.

8 oz (225 g) butter, softened
8 oz (225 g) sugar
4 eggs, separated
*about 1 lb (450 g) fresh walnuts
shelled and peeled*
1 dessertspoon rum (optional)
2-3 oz (60-85 g) bitter chocolate

In a bowl, cream together the butter and sugar until the mixture is light and
fluffy. Add the 4 egg yolks and blend well.

Powder, in a food processor, half of the walnuts. Chop roughly the
remaining ones. Fold both the powdered and chopped walnuts into the butter
and sugar mixture. Add the rum, if used. Beat the egg whites to soft peaks and
fold into the pudding. Pour into a lined tin about 10 in (25 cm) in diameter and
about 2 in (5 cm) deep. Chill for at least 12 hours.

To make the decoration cut the chocolate into pieces and place in a bowl
over hot water, and melt, then pour promptly over a smooth surface such as
marble or formica. Spread the chocolate thinly with a spatula and leave to cool
thoroughly, about 5 or 6 hours. Just before serving, invert the walnut pudding
onto a dish or a cake stand. Using a long metal spatula or a large kitchen knife,
make the chocolate curls: holding the utensil with both hands, and pressing
very hard, scrape the cooled chocolate, making large, irregular curls. Arrange
them, at random, on top and around the pudding.

Serves 8

RAISINÉ

This drink is made from freshly pressed grapes, either white or black, but muscat would be best for flavour. The champagne is an extra luxury which is optional, and slightly sparkling white wine like Gaillac would be a good alternative. The lemon juice enhances the flavour of the grapes, whichever sort you choose. I like to serve this with Tarte Tatin à Ma Façon, p116, or Gâteau aux Noix Solognote, p117.

2 lb (1 kg) grapes
juice of ½ lemon
1 tablespoon Crème de Cassis
1 bottle champagne or dry white wine

Prepare this drink at the last minute. Remove the grapes from the stalks, reserving a few small sprays, and press. (I use a vegetable mill with medium-size disc.) Strain the juice into a large jug. Add the lemon juice, Crème de Cassis and champagne or wine, give a good stir and serve with ice. Balance a grape spray on the rim of each glass for decoration.

Serves 4 generously

Raisiné, Tarte Tatin à ma Façon
Gâteau aux Noix Solognote

Desserts, Cakes, and Drinks

PICKLED QUINCES

These preserved quinces are very versatile. They are
delicious with smoked turkey, cold pork and duck. They
go well, too, with a mature Cheddar cheese, and the
Mustard Bread, p88.

6-7 quinces
15 fl oz (420 ml) cider vinegar
1½ lb (675 g) sugar
rind of one lemon
3 cloves
2 cinnamon sticks
1 in (2.5 cm) piece ginger root
1 allspice berry
2 vanilla pods

Put the vinegar, sugar and lemon rind in an enamelled saucepan. Put the
cloves, cinnamon sticks, ginger root and allspice in a muslin and add to the pan.
Heat until the sugar is dissolved, then cover and simmer for about 10 minutes.

Peel and core the quinces and cut each into 4. Add them to the pickling
liquid. Simmer for about an hour, or until the quinces are soft but still holding
their shape. Cool in the liquid.

Strain the quinces and place them in a clean preserving jar. Bring the spiced
liquid to a rapid boil and cook until reduced by half. Pour over the fruit, which
should be completely immersed. Place the two vanilla pods in the jar and cover
tightly. Keep a month before using.

Fills 1½ lb (675 g) jar

COLD SPICED TEA

Sweet spiced tea is particularly appreciated after
an Indian meal. For a change, replace the ginger with a
few peppercorns, and add a piece of dried orange peel.
Serve it at tea-time with Blueberry Hill, p108.

about 3 tablespoons sugar
1 vanilla pod
1 stick cinnamon
2 cloves
5-7 green cardamom pods
1 in (2.5 cm) piece fresh ginger root
1½-2 tablespoons Orange Pekoe tea
1-2 marigold flowers

In a saucepan, boil 2 pt (1 litre) of water. Take it off the heat and add the sugar,
vanilla, cinnamon, cloves, cardamom and ginger. Leave to infuse for at least 15
minutes, then add the tea. Return the saucepan to the heat and simmer for 5
minutes. Strain into a heatproof jug, let cool and chill.

Before serving, add ice, if you wish. Sprinkle a few petals on the top of the
jug, and keep some to decorate each glass. Place a cinnamon stick in each glass.

Makes 2 pts (1 litre)

SAGE WINE

In Provence this fortified wine is made with freshly dried
sage flowers. Sage leaves are a perfectly good substitute.
Ideally this wine should be matured for a year. Serve it
with Squirrel Treat, p115.

1 bottle (75 cl) red or rosé wine
3 tablespoon dried sage leaves
fruit spirit (Eau de Vie)
20 sugar lumps or 6 dessertspoons honey

Add 3 tablespoons of sage leaves to the wine, cork and macerate for a month,
shaking the bottle occasionally. Filter through muslin, add the spirit and sugar
(or honey) and stir until dissolved. Bottle, cork and store in a cool, dark place.

Serves 4-6

WINTER

Winter's cold calls for warmth: warm, elegant evening meals *à deux*, mid-week as a special tonic, or at the week-end. Week-ends also bring warmth on a different scale: house-guests, family and friends, and lingering brunches or teas that drift into invitations for impromptu suppers.

In winter, less opportunity for gardening and relaxing outdoors means more time for planning and carrying out delicious menus, and presenting them with, perhaps, slightly more preparation than one would give in summer. Large and hearty winter appetites may call for an increase in the size of portion, perhaps, but never crudity of presentation. Soups bring warmth, home-made pasta calls for lovely sauces, and home-made muffins provide the excuse to bring out all the home-made jams, preserves and butters from summer and autumn.

Chutneys and pickles preserved wild mushrooms and stored nuts can all be brought out with domestic and creative pride, to provide quick and easy meals or enhance the admittedly limited selection of fresh winter produce. Don't let this limited selection be an excuse for unimaginative food or boring meals. Broccoli, leeks, chicory, parsnips and celery are most flavoursome now, and deserve all the respect and attention to detail that one would give more exotic produce. Even the humble potato, cabbage, onion and carrot deserve renewed thought and effort.

Use ingenuity to overcome the limited choice of fresh fruit. Dried fruit are invaluable for winter meals, in fruit salads or as flavourings in other dishes, and they are tastier than out-of-season strawberries, for example. Citrus fruit are at their best now, and need no dressing up – a bowl of shiny clementines, with their dark green, glossy and aromatic leaves, is as elegant an end to a meal as one would wish for.

SPECKLED RIBBONS

The ribbons are in fact home-made pasta: paprika and
turmeric give them a rich orange colour and poppy seeds
give a contrasting, blue-black speckled effect. I use a hand-
operated pasta machine; the dough should be cut in 1 in
(2.5 cm) wide ribbons. This pasta is delicious with petit-
pois and with the Coriander Pesto, p147, or the Walnut
and Saffron Sauce, p146.

10 oz (280 g) wholemeal flour
3 large eggs, at room temperature
$^1/_2$ tablespoon olive oil
1 scant tablespoon poppy seeds
salt
$^1/_4$ teaspoon paprika
$^1/_4$ teaspoon turmeric

In a large bowl, place the flour in a mound. Make a well in the centre and add
the eggs, olive oil, poppy seeds, salt, paprika and turmeric. With a wooden
spoon, first mix together the wet ingredients, then begin to incorporate the
flour. When most of the flour has been absorbed, place the dough on a flat
surface, lightly floured, and start kneading. Continue working in the
remaining flour until it is all incorporated. Leave to rest for at least 20 minutes
or up to 3 hours.

Set the wheel for the rollers of the pasta machine at the widest setting. Take
about a quarter of the pasta and pass it through the plain rollers. Fold the
resulting rectangular strip in 3 so that the width remains the same, while the
length is a third of what it was. Sprinkle with flour and repeat the operation 10
to 12 times, until it is obvious to the eye that the dough has become a properly
smooth, homogeneous mixture. (These steps take the place of hand kneading.) Flour the table, and lay the first strip on it. Repeat the operation with the
rest of the dough.

Move the wheel to the next number, to bring the rollers a little closer. Now
pass the 4 sheets of dough, one by one, through the rollers. Then bring the
rollers closer together by turning the adjusting wheel. Every now and then it
will be necessary to cut the dough across in 2, because otherwise the sheets
become so long that they are difficult to handle. When the sheets are $^1/_{16}$ in
(1.5 mm) thick, lay them on a floured board, cover with a tea-cloth and leave to
rest for 10 to 15 minutes. Meanwhile, set a bamboo pole or a broom between
the backs of 2 chairs.

The pasta is now ready to be cut into wide ribbons. Make large folds with
each piece of dough, and cut in strips 1 in (2.5 cm) wide. Hang over the broom

handle or bamboo pole, making sure that the pasta ribbons do not overlap. Leave to dry until needed. If you do not need all the pasta, keep some – loosely piled – in the refrigerator, or even better, freeze for another time.

Bring to the boil a large pan filled with salted water. Immerse the pasta and cook for 50 seconds precisely. Drain, add some butter, oil or one of the sauces mentioned above and serve.

Serves 6-8

Speckled Ribbons, Coriander Pesto

Eggs, Cheeses and Grains

CORNMEAL AND CARAWAY MUFFINS

These are delicious eaten with a soup, such as Almond
and Parsnip Cream, p141, or an egg dish. They go well
too, served hot, with Celery and Bacon Wheels, p143. I
also serve them at tea time, split in two horizontally, with a
little piece of butter placed in the centre. The muffins may
be frozen, and reheated, without thawing first.

3 oz (85 g) unbleached flour
3 oz (85 g) medium cornmeal or polenta
1 teaspoon baking powder
1 teaspoon sugar
salt
1 teaspoon caraway seeds
1 teaspoon dried oregano or rosemary
4 tablespoons olive oil
1 large egg
6 fl oz (150 ml) milk

Preheat the oven to 400°F/200°C/Gas 6
Grease generously 12 muffin cups. Sift the flour, cornmeal or polenta,
baking powder, sugar and salt in a large bowl. Stir in the caraway seeds and
dried oregano (or rosemary).

In a small bowl, beat together the olive oil, egg and milk. Pour the liquid
mixture over the dried ingredients. With a wooden spoon, bind quickly, but
lightly, the 2 mixtures. Three-quarter fill the muffin cups, and bake for 20
minutes, then remove from the oven and invert on a cake rack. Leave for a few
minutes and serve hot with fresh butter.

Makes 12 muffins

Eggs, Cheeses and Grains

BRIOCHES DE PÂTES CHINOISES

Here six brioche moulds are used to shape the Chinese egg
noodles. In the ingredients, variations are many: the oil
could be a mixture of sesame and sunflower oil; the
herbs, a combination of parsley and oregano. The
brioches make a delicious accompaniment to Leeks and
Parma Ham, p139.

8 oz (225 g) thin egg noodles
1 oz (30 g) butter
2 tablespoons dry breadcrumbs
1 tablespoon olive oil
1 teaspoon fresh thyme or winter savory
2 heaped tablespoons fresh coriander, chopped
2 scant tablespoons pine-nuts or pistachios, lightly toasted
2 oz (60 g) herbed black olives
salt and freshly ground pepper
2 oz (60 g) grated Gruyère or Emmenthal cheese

Grease generously with the butter 6 medium-size brioche moulds. Sprinkle
with the breadcrumbs. Reserve.

Bring to the boil a large pan filled with salted water. Drop in the egg noodles
and immediately remove from the heat. In 6 minutes the noodles will be
perfectly cooked. Drain and transfer to a bowl. Toss in the olive oil, thyme or
winter savory, fresh coriander, pine-nuts (or pistachios) and the black olives,
stoned and chopped in fairly small pieces. Season with salt and pepper.

Fill each brioche mould with some of the noodles, and sprinkle with grated
cheese. Grill for 5 minutes.

Invert the moulded noodles onto a serving dish and serve immediately, with
perhaps a few coriander sprigs for garnish.

Makes 6 brioches

PRAWNS WITH BACON

Ideally jumbo prawns should be used and, though extravagantly expensive, I think they are worth buying for this dish. The combination of prawns and bacon works well, and the sage imparts a complementary fragrance. Serve with Moules Farçies, p130, or with steamed mange-touts or tiny petit-pois.

12 jumbo prawns
6 slices lean bacon
12-24 sage leaves
1 tablespoon cognac

Carefully peel the prawns, leaving the heads and tails intact. Devein the prawns and marinate for an hour in the cognac, tossing the prawns once or twice during that time.

Drain and wrap each prawn in half a bacon slice, sliding the sage between the prawns and bacon. Place, seam down, on a metal rack and grill for about 5 minutes. Serve them immediately.

Serves 6-12

Prawns with Bacon, Moules Farçies
Cold Sorrel Sauce

MOULES FARÇIES

In this recipe, the mussel shells are filled with a herbed mussel stuffing. The shells are tied closed with a piece of string or raffia; each guest opens the mussels on his or her plate. Reserve only the largest shells. If you can get some seaweed or samphire from your fishmonger, use it to garnish the dish. Prawns with Bacon, p128, and Cold Sorrel Sauce, p146, would add to the seafood theme.

2 lb (1 kg) mussels
2 oz (60 g) butter
1-2 spring onions or white of 1 leek
1 tablespoon olive oil
about 4 tablespoons fresh breadcrumbs
a little parsley, chopped
salt and freshly ground pepper
1-2 saffron stigmas (optional)

Discard any broken mussels and scrub the rest under cold water, using a small brush. Pull away any beards and, using a sharp knife, scrape off any barnacles. Discard any mussel which remains open, when lightly tapped.

Place the mussels in a large pan, cover and leave over high heat for 5 minutes or until the shells are all open, shaking the pan once or twice.

Drain the mussels over a bowl, reserving their liquor, which can be used for a soup. Discard any shell which has remained closed. Remove the flesh with kitchen tongs and chop it, taking care not to break the shells' hinges.

Using half the butter, sauté the chopped spring onions or white part of a leek, until softened. Add to the mussel flesh.

Heat the remaining butter and oil together, and fry the breadcrumbs until golden. Drain on absorbent paper, and stir, along with the parsley, salt and pepper, into the mussel mixture.

If you are using the saffron, grind it in a mortar and add it to the stuffing, scrupulously scraping off every particle.

Select about 20 mussels shells, choosing the largest ones. Fill each shell, using a small spoon, with some of the stuffing. Tie each mussel closed with a piece of string or raffia.

Arrange on a flat dish, using seaweed and any pretty shells or sea decoration you have, such as coral, for presentation.

Serves 4-6

SARDINE CRACKERS

This dish is so called as sardines are wrapped in paper thin
filo dough, then rolled and shaped like a cracker. The best
way to deal with the pastry is to work one sheet at a time,
leaving the rest covered with a damp cloth or a plastic bag
so the sheets don't become brittle and difficult to work. I
buy filo dough from Greek grocers or good delicatessens.
Use the best brand of sardines, the type preserved in olive
oil and imported from Spain; each tin contains about six
sardines and you will need half a sheet of filo dough for
each one. If you don't use all the filo dough, freeze the
remainder for later use. Serve, if you like, with Radicchio,
Corn Salad and Cheese, p142, or the Crisp Potato Skins,
p136, and Walnut and Saffron Sauce, p146.

3 tins sardines (about 18 sardines)
1/2 lemon, thinly sliced
a few fennel seeds
about 10 sheets filo dough
4 oz (120 g) butter

Preheat the oven to 375°F/190°C/Gas 5
Drain the sardines. Make a slit lengthways in each sardine using a sharp knife,
and remove the backbone. Scrap off some of the skin. Push half a lemon slice
into the slit. Sprinkle with fennel seeds and reserve.

Make 2 'crackers' at a time: take a sheet of pastry and lay it flat on a board.
Divide in 2, crossways, and brush lightly with melted butter, leaving out 2
strips either side of the sheet, about 2 in (5 cm) from the edges, where the
'crackers' will be pinched and twisted half a turn. Place a sardine at the end of
each strip and roll, then pinch and twist. Repeat the operation until all the
sardines and pastry sheets are used.

Place the 'crackers' on a greased oven tray and brush each one with more
butter. Bake for 25 to 30 minutes or until crisp and golden. Serve immediately.

Serves 6-9

Meat

Sweet and Sour Lamb Fillets

For this light lamb dish, I usually get short lamb fillets,
allowing one per person, which is quite generous. The
cumin imparts a complementary and unusual flavour to
the meat. Serve with Galettes de Pomme de Terre, p144
or Vegetables Indian Fashion, p135.

4-6 lamb fillets
2 tablespoons olive oil
1 heaped teaspoon powdered cumin
juice and rind of 1/2 lemon
salt and freshly ground pepper
about 2 tablespoons runny honey
4-6 Chinese cabbage leaves
rind of 1 orange, cut into thin strips

To make the marinade combine the olive oil, cumin, lemon juice, salt and
pepper. Pour over the fillets. Leave for 3 to 4 hours to marinate, or up to 48
hours in the refrigerator, turning the meat from time to time.

Preheat the grill to high. Drain the fillets, and pat dry. Spread the honey all
over the fillets and grill for 4 to 5 minutes on each side, or until slightly
caramelized and a deep amber colour. Turn off the grill, leaving the fillets to
continue cooking for 10 minutes. By that time the lamb will have cooked but
still be pink in the centre. Slice each fillet and arrange on a Chinese cabbage
leaf. Serve garnished with thin strips of orange and lemon peel.

Serves 4-6

Meat

VEAL ESCALOPES WITH PAPRIKA

For this dish the thickness of the veal is important, so ask
your butcher to flatten the scallops as thinly as possible.
You can replace the pink yams with potatoes, but they will
lack that sweetness which goes so well with paprika. Serve
with Vegetables Indian Fashion, p135, and Carrot and
Broccoli Purées, p138.

6 large veal escalopes
1 tablespoon olive oil
1 fennel bulb
1 teaspoon paprika
1 tablespoon strong Dijon mustard
6 bacon rashers, thinly sliced
1 small pink yam, peeled and sliced thinly
salt
8 fl oz (225 ml) sour cream

Preheat the oven to 350°F/180°C/Gas 4

In a heavy pan, heat the oil and sauté the fennel, trimmed and sliced
lengthways. (Reserve some of the feathery fronds for garnish.) When it is soft
on the outside, but still 'al dente' in the centre, remove from the heat and stir in
the paprika. Reserve.

Spread each escalope evenly with some of the mustard : place a bacon rasher
on top, then a yam slice. Season with salt. Roll the escalopes and secure them
with a cocktail stick.

Transfer the fennel and paprika mixture to an oblong, ovenproof dish, large
enough to hold the 6 veal rolls. Place the escalopes on top. Pour over a glass of
water, cover and bake for about 30 minutes.

Arrange the veal rolls and fennel on a serving dish. Add the sour cream to the
juice and vegetables in the dish and bring to a boil. Pour over the escalopes,
sprinkle with more paprika and garnish with the fennel fronds. Serve
immediately.

Serves 6

VEGETABLES INDIAN FASHION

I always keep a small bottle of olive oil flavoured with two or three garlic cloves. It is very handy for many dishes and salad dressings, and gives you just a subtle awareness of the garlic. Here the cumin seeds are fried briefly first, for an unusual fragrance. Serve with Sweet and Sour Lamb Fillets (p132) or Veal Escalopes with Paprika (p133).

2 garlic cloves, peeled and cut in 2
3-4 tablespoons oil
3 carrots
3 potatoes, boiled and peeled
2 scant teaspoons cumin seeds
10 shallots, peeled
8 oz (225 g) frozen, minted peas
1 teaspoon turmeric
a little sugar
salt
juice of 1 lemon

Steep the garlic cloves in the oil for an hour or so.
Peel and cube the carrots and dice the cooked potatoes. Heat the oil (discarding the garlic), and fry the cumin seeds, letting them sizzle for a few seconds. Add the peeled shallots and carrots and cook for 15 to 20 minutes. The shallots should be translucent, but not browned; the carrots still firm.

Add the potatoes, peas, turmeric and sugar. Season with salt. Cook gently for a further 5 minutes. Take off the heat, pour over the lemon juice, tossing the vegetables. Transfer to a serving dish and serve at once.

Serve 5-6

Vegetables Indian Fashion, Veal Escalopes
with Paprika served with Carrot and
Broccoli Purées, Sweet and Sour
Lamb Fillets

CRISP POTATO SKINS

These are cooked twice: first baked in the oven, then deep fried. I like to serve them with plenty of sour cream and chives. Place the potato dish in the centre of the dining table and let the guests pick up the crispy skins with their fingers, dipping the skins into the sauce. Radicchio, Corn Salad and Cheese, p142, makes a good accompaniment, its slight bitterness contrasting with the rich flavour of the potato skins and sauce. Walnut and Saffron Sauce, p146, is nice for dipping, too.

6 large potatoes
a few chives
10 fl oz (280 ml) sour cream
oil for deep frying
salt and freshly ground pepper

Preheat the oven to 350°F/180°C/Gas 4
Bake the cleaned, whole potatoes for about an hour, depending on their size. Meanwhile, finely chop most of the chives and add them to the sour cream. Reserve. When the potatoes are ready, put heatproof gloves on, and cut the potatoes in 2. Scoop out most of the flesh (reserving it for a purée or a soup), then cut each half again into 3 wedges. Deep-fry the skins until golden and very crisp. Drain on kitchen paper. Season and garnish with a few whole chives. Serve immediately in a wicker basket or dish lined with a napkin.

Serve 6

Crisp Potato Skins, Sardine Crackers,
Walnut and Saffron Sauce,
Radicchio, Corn Salad and Cheese

CARROT AND BROCCOLI PURÉES

These two purées go well together, in both taste and
colour. I serve them on the same dish making alternating
colours of orange and green. The potatoes give body to the
vegetables. Serve the purées with Veal Escalopes
with Paprika, p133.

1 lb (450 g) large carrots, peeled and halved
8 oz (225 g) broccoli, divided into large florets
2 large potatoes
10 fl oz (225 ml) sour cream
2 oz (60 g) butter
nutmeg
salt and freshly ground pepper

Halve the potatoes and steam them for about 20 minutes, the carrots for 15
minutes and the broccoli for 10 minutes. When the broccoli is ready, cool
quickly under cold running water to preserve its emerald green colour.

In a food processor, put half the sour cream and half the butter, add some
nutmeg, salt and pepper and a potato, cubed. Process for a few seconds only.
Add the broccoli and process until thoroughly blended then transfer to a bowl.
Repeat the operation with the carrots and the remaining ingredients to make
the carrot purée. If not served immediately, cover with foil and re-heat in a
moderate oven. Serve hot, in small scoops.

Serves 6-8

Vegetables and Salads

LEEKS AND PARMA HAM

The leeks are wrapped in transparently thin Parma ham
slices, so a little of their delicate green colour shows
through. Serve with Brioches de Pâtes Chinoises,
p127, and Galettes de Pomme de Terre, p144.

8 small leeks
8 very thin Parma ham slices
a little olive oil
coarsely ground black peppercorns (optional)

Trim, top and bottom, the leeks, then slit them halfway and rinse under cold
running water to remove every trace of soil and grit. Steam for 10 to 12
minutes. Cool immediately under cold running water.

Remove a dark green outer leaf and cut it into thin strands. Reserve. Wrap
each leek half with a Parma ham slice. Wet the tip of your fingers with oil and
rub it over the ham. This will make it moist and slightly translucent. Scatter
over the coarsely ground peppercorns, if using, and place the reserved leek
strands in a pretty pattern on top, then serve.

Serve 6-8

ALMOND AND PARSNIP CREAM

This is a rich and warming soup to serve with Leeks and
Parma Ham, p139, and Dried Fruit Salad, p149. I use a
scooped-out Savoy cabbage as a tureen.

1 pt (550 ml) milk
1 pt (550 ml) light stock
7 oz (200 g) ground almonds
a pinch of mace
1 bay leaf
1 lb (450 g) parsnips, peeled and roughly chopped
1 Savoy cabbage (optional)
4 fl oz (120 ml) sour cream (optional)
salt and freshly ground pepper
2 oz (60 g) blanched almonds, toasted

Bring to the boil the milk, stock, ground almonds, mace, bay leaf and parsnips.
Lower the heat and simmer for 20 minutes.

Meanwhile, carefully scoop the central portion from a Savoy cabbage (if
using) leaving several layers of outer leaves intact.

Purée the soup through the fine mesh of a vegetable mouli, adding a little
sour cream if you find the mixture too thick. Season, re-heat, then pour
carefully into the scooped-out cabbage or a soup tureen. Garnish with lightly
toasted almonds, then serve.

Serves 6

*Almond and Parsnip Cream, Celery and
Bacon Wheels, Cornmeal and
Caraway Muffins*

RADICCHIO, CORN SALAD AND CHEESE

This salad is as delicious as it looks. The slight bitterness of red chicory or radicchio, counteracts the richness of the cheeses, and the crunchy pistachios contrast with the smoothness. This salad goes well with Sardine Crackers, p131, Crisp Potato Skins, p136, and Walnut and Saffron Sauce, p146.

2-3 heads of red chicory (radicchio)
4 oz (120 g) corn salad
salt and pepper
about 10 green peppercorns
juice of 1/2 lemon
3 tablespoons walnut oil
a few pistachio nuts
4 oz (120 g) Stilton cheese
4 oz (120 g) Double Gloucester cheese

Trim off the stems from the red chicory. Pull out the leaves (discarding any blemished ones) and wash. Drain and pat dry.

Cut off the root ends of the corn salad, and clean scrupulously. Drain and dry thoroughly.

In a small bowl, place some salt, freshly ground pepper and the green peppercorns, lightly crushed. Add the lemon juice and beat in the walnut oil. Stir in the pistachio nuts. Trim off the rinds, if necessary, from the 2 cheeses. Crumble coarsely the Stilton, and grate the Double Gloucester with a medium-size grid.

To assemble: in a large, shallow bowl, add the dressing to the red chicory and corn salad and toss well. Gently fold in the 2 cheeses and serve.

Serves 6

CELERY AND BACON WHEELS

The head of celery is filled between the stalks with a bacon
and Stilton mixture and cut across to make wheels. Serve
with Cornmeal and Caraway Muffins, p126, and Almond
and Parsnip Cream, p141, for a light lunch, or, for a
snack, with the Prawns with Bacon, p128.

4 bacon slices
1 head of celery
4 oz (120 g) Stilton or Roquefort cheese
4 oz (120 g) cream cheese
a few chives, finely chopped
a little paprika
a pinch of cayenne pepper

In a heavy pan, sauté the bacon, without adding any fat, until crisp. Drain on
absorbent paper and crumble in tiny pieces.

Trim, top and bottom, the head of celery, discarding, if necessary,
blemished outer stalks. Clean under cold running water and let drip upside
down for a few minutes. Pat dry.

In a small bowl, mash together the Stilton or Roquefort, cream cheese,
finely chopped chives, paprika and cayenne pepper. Add the bacon pieces and
check that the seasoning is right. Open the head of celery carefully, without
breaking the stalks, and fill each with the cream cheese mixture (I do this with a
small spoon). The filling should be spread the length of the celery. Wrap
tightly in foil and refrigerate for about 2 hours, or longer if you like. This will
firm the filling and make the final operation easy.

Unwrap the celery and, with a heavy knife, cut across in slices. Place,
slightly overlapping, on a shallow dish, and serve.

Makes 12 slices

GALETTES DE POMME DE TERRE

These are flat cakes made with potatoes and leeks – golden and crisp outside, moist inside. As they are quite rich, serve simply with Leeks and Parma Ham, p139, or a green salad and a light pudding.

5 large potatoes
3 medium-size leeks
1 teaspoon butter
2 tablespoons lard
salt and freshly ground pepper
1 teaspoon dry thyme

Peel and wash the potatoes, then grate or cut into matchstick size. Squeeze dry and reserve.

Trim the leeks, cutting away the green part (this may be used to flavour a stock). Remove the outer leaf from each leek and wash well. Drain the leeks and chop them fairly finely. Melt the butter in a heavy saucepan, and gently cook the leeks until reduced a little and softened. Reserve.

Melt some lard in a 5 in (12.5 cm) sauté pan or, even better, in an omelette pan. Using a wooden spoon, spread a thin layer of potatoes in the pan, season with salt and pepper, and sprinkle with a little thyme, crushing it in the palm of your hand to release the aromatic oil from the leaf cells. Cover with a thin layer of leeks, then finish with more remaining potatoes – a quarter of the ingredients should have been used. Season again. Reduce the heat and cook gently for 10 minutes. Carefully invert the galette onto a flat dish of similar size, then slide back into the pan to cook the other side for a further 10 to 15 minutes. Transfer to a shallow dish and keep warm while you repeat the operation with the remaining ingredients three times. Serve hot.

Makes 4 galettes

Galettes de Pomme de Terre, Leeks and Parma Ham, Brioches de Pâtes Chinoises

Sauces

WALNUT AND SAFFRON SAUCE

This sauce can be served either hot or at room temperature. It goes well with Sardine Crackers, p131, Radicchio, Corn Salad and Cheese, p142, and Crisp Potato Skins, p136.

8 oz (225 g) cream cheese
5 fl oz (150 ml) creamed smatana or Greek yoghurt
1 tablespoon walnut oil
4-5 saffron stigmas
5 oz (150 g) walnuts, toasted and ground
a few chives
salt and white pepper
paprika

In a bowl, beat together the cream cheese, creamed smatana or Greek yoghurt, and walnut oil until thoroughly blended. Grind the saffron in a mortar and stir it into the sauce. Add the ground walnuts. Chop in a few chives, reserving a few for the garnish. Season.

Transfer the sauce to a bowl. Place parallel strips of paper over the surface, and dust liberally with paprika. Carefully remove the paper, place the reserved chives on top, and serve.

Makes 8 fl oz (225 ml)

◆

COLD SORREL SAUCE

Serve with Prawns with Bacon, p128, steamed potatoes, or as a dressing for mixed or tomato salads. You can substitute watercress for the sorrel.

1 bunch sorrel leaves, about 3 oz (85 g)
2 hard-boiled eggs, sliced
1 teaspoon strong Dijon Mustard
about 6 tablespoons olive oil
juice of 1/2 lemon
salt and freshly ground pepper

Cut off most of the sorrel stalks, then coarsely chop the leaves. Place in a food processor, and process until finely chopped. Add the sliced eggs, turning the motor on and off. Add the mustard, then, with the motor still running, the olive oil in a thin stream. Lastly, add the lemon juice. Season to taste and process again for a few seconds. You should have a smooth, pale green sauce, with a sharp, refreshing taste. Garnish, if wished, with a few thin strips of sorrel, then serve.

Makes 8 fl oz (225 ml)

CORIANDER PESTO

This is my version of the Italian basil pesto. Here an entire bunch of coriander leaves is used, giving a very aromatic sauce. It can be made in double or triple quantity for freezing, but it's best to omit the cheese and butter, and add them to the pesto after thawing. As a variation, replace the olive oil with walnut oil and omit the garlic. Serve this sauce with Speckled Ribbons, p124.

1 bunch fresh, cleaned coriander, stalks removed
6 fl oz (180 ml) fruity olive oil
2 tablespoons pine-nuts, lightly toasted
1 purple garlic clove, lightly crushed
1 teaspoon salt
2 oz (60 g) Parmesan cheese, freshly grated
1 oz (30 g) Cheddar cheese, freshly grated
2 oz (60 g) butter, softened

In a blender, place the coriander leaves roughly chopped, olive oil, pine-nuts, garlic clove and salt. Process at high speed, cutting off the motor once or twice, in order to scrape down the ingredients.

When the sauce is well blended, transfer it to a bowl and add the freshly grated Parmesan and Cheddar cheeses. When well incorporated, beat in the softened butter and serve.

Makes 10 fl oz (280 ml)

Dried Fruit Salad, Toast Water,
Parsley Tisane, Hazelnut butter

DRIED FRUIT SALAD

In this salad I included the little-known Hunza apricots;
they are untreated wild apricots from Afghanistan with a
more scented and milder taste than the ordinary dried
apricots. The kernel inside is delicious, too, and not bitter.
I find them in health food shops. Serve with Toast Water,
p157, or Parsley Tisane, p157, for an unusual and
refreshing end to a meal.

8 oz (225 g) Hunza apricots
8 oz (225 g) dried apricots
8 oz (225 g) giant Californian prunes
2 pts (1 litre) jasmine or China tea
1-2 vanilla pods
a few cardamon pods
1 pomegranate

Soak the Hunza and dried apricots and the prunes in the hot tea, placing
amongst them the vanilla pods and cardamon seeds, removed from their pods.
Leave for a couple of hours, or even better, overnight.

Stone the Hunza apricots and the prunes. Break the apricot stones open,
remove the inner kernels and add them to the fruit. Remove the skin and all the
white membranes from the pomegranate and add the red translucent kernels
to the dried fruits. Serve the salad chilled, or at room temperature. For the
sake of colour, you may want to add a small handful of currants. The salad will
keep for several days.

Serves 6

TULIP BISCUITS

These biscuits are tulip shaped, thus making little cups in
which ice creams or sorbets can be served, so that content
and container are eaten. I use muffin or brioche moulds to
form the biscuits, but, failing these, small glasses
placed upside down will do, too. The tulips will keep for
weeks in airtight tins.

2 egg whites
4 oz (120 g) castor sugar
2 oz (60 g) plain flour
½ teaspoon vanilla essence
2 oz (60 g) butter, melted and cooled slightly

Preheat the oven to 400°F/200°C/Gas 6
In a bowl beat together the egg whites and castor sugar, using a fork. Add the
flour, vanilla essence and butter. Spread the mixture on greased baking sheets,
making circles about 5 in (12.5 cm) in diameter.

   Bake for 5-7 minutes. When the biscuits are a pale gold colour, lift them
carefully and place inside muffin moulds, brioche moulds or over upside-
down glasses. Shape the edges promptly to make the frill. Cool. Store
immediately in airtight tins.

Makes about 12 biscuits

Tulip Biscuits filled with Prune and Port Ice
Cream and Cranberry Sorbet,
accompanied by fresh cranberries

CRANBERRY SORBET

Cranberries have a sharp, refreshing taste, so this sorbet
would be nice to end a rather rich meal. Sorbets should be
eaten within a day of making, as opposed to ice creams,
which improve after that period of time. Serve in Tulip
Biscuits, p150, and for a special meal, alternate the
cranberry sorbet with Prune and Port Ice Cream p153.

1 lb (450 g) cranberries
12 oz (340 g) sugar
juice of 1 orange

In a saucepan, slowly heat 1 pt (550 ml) water and the sugar, stirring, until the
sugar has dissolved. Raise the heat and when the syrup starts boiling, add the
cranberries, and allow to cool.

Sieve the cranberries and syrup and place the purée in a blender along with
the orange juice. Blend at high speed, then transfer to a metal tray. Freeze for 2
to 3 hours. Return the mushy mixture to the blender and blend for 3 minutes.
It will become cream-like and frothy. Return the mixture to the freezer for
another 2 hours or up to 24 hours. An hour before serving place the sorbet in
the refrigerator to allow it to soften.

Serves 8

Desserts and Cakes

PRUNE AND PORT ICE CREAM

Here the combination of prunes and port works well. I
use, for steeping the prunes, a fragrant China tea, such as
Lapsang Souchong or Oolong. The stones may be broken
open to release the kernel inside and then placed on top of
the ice cream. To prevent the cream graining during
beating, add one tablespoon of iced water (I do this by
leaving an ice cube to melt into a spoon). You can also
place the bowl, beaters and cream in the freezer
for 10 minutes. Serve, scooped out, in light-coloured
Tulip Biscuits, p150, to contrast with the dark rich colour
of the ice cream.

1 lb (450 g) large prunes
2 pt (1 litre) China tea
1 vanilla pod
about 2 oz (60 g) sugar
1 tablespoon port
4 fl oz (120 ml) double cream, lightly whipped

Soak the prunes in the China tea with the vanilla pod for 2 to 3 hours or, even
better overnight.

Drain the prunes and stone, reserving both the juice and the kernels. Purée
the prunes, adding a little of the juice if necessary – the mixture should be firm
but not thick. Stir in the sugar and port. Fold in the lightly whipped cream.
Test for sweetness and freeze.

When the mixture begins to set, beat well once more. Return the mixture to
the freezer. About 30 minutes before serving, transfer the ice cream to the
refrigerator to soften slightly.

Serves 6

ORANGE AND HAZELNUT CAKE

This moist, nutty cake will keep well for a week or so, and
in fact it improves after a day or two. Serve it at tea-time.

10 oz (280 g) brown sugar
5 oz (150 g) butter
8 fl oz (225 ml) milk
3 large eggs, separated
1 teaspoon vanilla essence
8 oz (225 g) wholemeal flour
2 teaspoons baking powder
1/2 teaspoon salt
4 oz (120 g) hazelnuts, toasted,
skins removed and roughly chopped
4 oz (120 g) raisins
grated rinds of 2 oranges
a little redcurrant jelly
1 lb (450 g) marzipan
3 glacé cherries
2 in (5 cm) piece crystallized angelica
silvered sugar balls

Preheat the oven to 250°F/180°C/Gas 4

Blend the sugar and butter until light in texture. Add the milk, egg yolks and vanilla. Sift together the flour, baking powder and salt. Add to the butter/sugar mixture. Stir in the hazelnuts, raisins and grated orange rinds. Fold in the stiffly beaten egg whites. Pour into a lined and greased, 8 in (20 cm) diameter tin. Bake for about 1 hour or until a skewer comes out clean when inserted in the centre of the cake. Transfer to a rack. Melt a little redcurrant jelly and brush it all over the cake, then leave to cool.

Meanwhile, roll out half the marzipan, between 2 pieces of waxed paper, into an approximately 8 in (20 cm) diameter circle. Using the cake tin, cut a neat circle with a sharp knife and place it on top of the cake. Roll out the remaining marzipan into a thinner layer. Using heart-shaped cutters, cut out 14 medium-size hearts, 1 large heart and 1 small heart. Place on the top of the cake, the large, a medium and finally the small heart, their 3 points meeting. Place the remaining hearts, upright, on the sides of the cake. (Use the redcurrant jelly to 'stick' them to the cake.)

Divide the glacé cherries in 2. Cut the angelica into small squares. Place them around the superimposed hearts. Push a silver ball in the centre curve of each heart, and around the large heart. Stud the glacé cherries and crystallized angelica with more silver balls.

Orange and Hazelnut Cake

Hazelnut Butter

'Butter' is the old-fashioned name for preserves normally
made with fruit purée and sugar. They have been used for
centuries and are associated with early American settlers.
Here I use hazelnut and cocoa, which gives a praliné taste
to the butter. It can be made into a sauce for ice creams or
puddings by adding the same quantity of cream, or
served, as it is, with freshly made melba toast.

8 oz (225 g) hazelnuts
4 oz (120 g) sugar
1 heaped teaspoon cocoa powder
1 generous tablespoon hazelnut or sunflower oil

Place the hazelnuts on a metal tray and toast for about 10 minutes in an oven at
350°F/180°C/Gas 4.

Let cool for a few minutes, then, with heatproof gloves on, rub off the skins,
winnowing the flakes over the sink by blowing gently.

Put the hazelnuts in a food processor and process until finely ground. Add
the sugar, cocoa powder and oil, and process until the mixture forms a ball.

Transfer to a jam pot. The hazelnut butter will keep for weeks, but it is a
good idea to store it in a cool place.

Makes 12 oz (340 g)

Drinks

PARSLEY TISANE

Parsley has excellent digestive properties and is rich in iron, calcium and vitamins. This infusion can be drunk instead of tea or coffee. It has a fresh clean taste and is tinted the faintest delicate green.

about 1 oz (30 g) parsley
honey (optional)

Boil 1 pt (550 ml) water and then pour it over the parsley and leave to infuse for 5 to 10 minutes. Drink hot or cold, sweetened with honey if you like.

Serves 3-4

TOAST WATER

This water was given to invalids in Victorian times. However, I remember once seeing Georgian silver toast-water jugs in an English country house. Perhaps toast water was inspired by Kvas, a Russian drink dating from the sixteenth century, made with yeast and rye bread or flour, and left to ferment. Kvas is still made nowadays. Whatever the origin of Toast Water, I think it is a good way to make London tap water nice tasting.

6 slices white bread

Toast the bread until a dark golden colour and quite hard, but don't burn the toast or it will impart a disagreeable flavour to the water. Place the toast in a jug and pour over 2 pt (1 litre) cold water. Let soak for an hour and strain into a clean jug. Serve chilled.

Serves 6

INDEX